IMAGES
of America

NEW JERSEY'S LINDBERGH
KIDNAPPING AND TRIAL

IMAGES
of America

NEW JERSEY'S LINDBERGH KIDNAPPING AND TRIAL

Mark W. Falzini and James Davidson

ARCADIA
PUBLISHING

Published by Arcadia Publishing
Charleston, South Carolina

Library of Congress Control Number: 2012940896

For all general information, please contact Arcadia Publishing:
Telephone 843-853-2070
Fax 843-853-0044
E-mail sales@arcadiapublishing.com
For customer service and orders:
Toll-Free 1-888-313-2665

Visit us on the Internet at www.arcadiapublishing.com

Mark Falzini dedicates this book to Oliver Sissman,
Gregg Senko, and Matthew Cornetto.

James G. Davidson dedicates this book to Dawn, James, and Tory.

CONTENTS

ACKNOWLEDGMENTS

The New Jersey State Police Museum and Learning Center is the repository of the largest collection of documents, photographs, and videos pertaining to the Lindbergh Kidnapping Case and the hub of research on that case. We wish to thank the members of the New Jersey State Police for their support and encouragement that helped to make this book possible, especially the superintendent, Col. Joseph "Rick" Fuentes, and the enlisted members assigned to the museum: Sgt. Frank Boyd, Sgt. Gabriel Rodriguez, Trooper I Adam Grossman, and Trooper I Philip Buck.

The support and encouragement of the State Police Memorial Association (SPMA), which serves as the board of trustees for the museum and learning center, is also greatly appreciated. The introduction to this book is based in part on the *New Jersey State Police Museum Teacher's Guide*, which was published by the SPMA in 1996.

We also wish to thank our editor at Arcadia Publishing, Erin Rocha, and our marketing director, P.J. Norlander, who tolerated our countless phone calls and e-mails and worked diligently to ensure that this book was published.

In addition to the aforementioned New Jersey State Police Museum, other organizations graciously shared their photograph collections with us. We are grateful to Jack Koppel of the Hopewell Township Historical Society, Ruth Luse of the *Hopewell Herald*, Terry McNealy of the Hunterdon County Historical Society, Stephanie Stevens of the Hunterdon County Cultural and Heritage Commission, Beverly Weidl of the Hopewell Museum, Cynthia Harris of the Jersey City Free Public Library Jersey Room, and Eileen Morales of the Historical Society of Princeton.

Several individuals shared either their personal photograph collections or their vast knowledge of the Lindbergh Case with us. They include Lloyd Gardner, Oliver Sissman, Adam Schrager, Alberta Hausenbauer, Richard Sloan, Dolores Raisch, Siglinde Rach, Richard Cahill, Kurt Tolksdorf, Michael Melsky, Kevin Klein, Michael Warmington, Robert Hauck, and Harry Kazman.

Lastly, we would like to thank our families. Without their support, encouragement, patience, and tolerance, this book could not have been written.

INTRODUCTION

In 1927, the American people were in desperate need of a hero. Our nation was suffering through the moral and political corruption brought about by Prohibition and the exploits of organized crime. There was a sense of hopelessness in an age where virtues such as honesty, courage, and pride in achievements seemed impossible to recognize. Charles A. Lindbergh never planned to be a hero when he decided to accept the challenge of a French businessman named Raymond Orteig.

Charles Lindbergh was a young airmail pilot who, at the age of 25, decided to compete for the first nonstop flight between New York and Paris. Others had tried before him, meeting failure and even death. On May 20, 1927, fighting heavy odds and bad weather, Lindbergh took off from Roosevelt Field in New York in his monoplane, named the *Spirit of St. Louis*. He flew alone, nonstop, across the Atlantic Ocean for 33 1/2 hours before landing at Le Bourget Field in Paris, France, on May 21, 1927. His daring accomplishment won him not only the $25,000 prize but also worldwide recognition and fame. It cost him, however, a loss of privacy that would last a lifetime.

Following his famous flight, Charles Lindbergh made many goodwill flights to set new records and advance the cause of civilian aviation. He was invited to Mexico by the American ambassador, Dwight Morrow, in an attempt to improve the strained relations between the United States and Mexico. It was on this tour that he met the ambassador's daughter, Anne Morrow.

Charles Lindbergh and Anne Morrow began dating and were eventually married in a private ceremony at her parents' home in Englewood, New Jersey, on May 27, 1929. Their first child, a son, was born on Anne's 24th birthday, June 22, 1930. They named him Charles A. Lindbergh Jr.

In the winter of 1932, the young family had not quite settled in their newly built home near Hopewell, New Jersey, when their lives would change forever. On the evening of March 1, 1932, Charles A. Lindbergh Jr. was kidnapped as he slept in his nursery crib. Several clues were left behind, including a ransom note, a homemade three-section ladder, and a chisel. That night, the New Jersey State Police began their investigation into the crime that shocked and outraged America and the world.

An intermediary named John F. Condon entered the case after a newspaper ran an editorial offering his assistance and met with the kidnapper on two occasions. In all, 15 ransom notes were received during the course of the negotiations. Eventually, Charles Lindbergh paid the $50,000 ransom demanded in the original ransom note, believing this was the only way to get his son back. Following the instructions of the kidnapper, the ransom was handed over by Condon on April 2, 1932, in a Bronx cemetery. While the money was not marked, the serial numbers of these bills, most of which were gold certificates, were carefully listed, although this fact was not made public.

After the ransom was paid, Charles Lindbergh was given instructions on where to find his son, but the search was in vain. On May 12, 1932, William Allen, a local truck driver, and his driving partner Orville Wilson discovered the child's body in the woods approximately five miles from Lindbergh's home.

Investigators from the New Jersey State Police, the Bureau of Investigation (known later—and referred to throughout this book—as the Federal Bureau of Investigation, or FBI) and the US Treasury Department were busy pursuing every possible lead. In addition, analysis of the wood used in the construction of the kidnap ladder would offer valuable clues once a suspect was apprehended. Handwriting experts carefully examined the 15 ransom notes, and this, too, would prove informative and revealing.

In September 1934, at a New York service station, a man paid for his gasoline with a $10 gold certificate. The United States had officially gone off the gold standard in May 1933, and the station attendant did not want to risk the bank refusing the gold certificate. For this reason, he wrote the purchaser's license number on the $10 bill. This lead broke the case when an alert bank teller notified the authorities of the gold certificate. The serial number matched with one that appeared on the list of Lindbergh ransom money serial numbers. The license number was traced to Bruno Richard Hauptmann, who lived in the Bronx section of New York.

Richard Hauptmann was a German immigrant who was in the United States illegally. Until April 1932, he had worked as a carpenter, after which time he focused on trading stocks. When Hauptmann was arrested on September 19, 1934, another ransom bill was found in his wallet. The following day, over $13,000 of the ransom was discovered in Hauptmann's garage. A floorboard in Hauptmann's attic was found to match the wood used for one of the rails in the kidnap ladder. Handwriting samples were taken from Hauptmann and experts hired by the state claimed his writing matched the writing of the ransom notes. In October, he was extradited from New York to Flemington, New Jersey, to be tried in the state and county in which the crime occurred.

Richard Hauptmann's trial began on January 2, 1935, in Flemington, New Jersey. Physical evidence as well as expert and eyewitness testimony directly connected him to the ladder, the handwriting in the ransom notes, and possession of the ransom money. The evidence and testimony presented at the six-week trial led to Hauptmann's conviction of murder during the commission of a felony. The sentence was death by electrocution.

Following unsuccessful appeals and a controversial intervention by New Jersey governor Harold G. Hoffman, Bruno Richard Hauptmann was executed in Trenton, New Jersey, on April 3, 1936.

While the Lindbergh Case is officially closed, to many historians and enthusiasts, it will never close. The Lindbergh Case is riddled with contradictions and unanswered questions, and every attempt to answer one question will often generate even more.

This book does not attempt to answer those questions or to put forth any new theories. However, the authors hope that by presenting a basic, straightforward narrative of the case, this book will capture the interest of those who are as yet unfamiliar with the Lindbergh Kidnapping Case and inspire them to learn more. It is also their hope that the unique photographs and captions herein will be of interest to those who are already knowledgeable of the case and help them to better understand the world of New Jersey's Lindbergh Kidnapping Crime and Trial.

One

THE HERO

At 10:00 p.m. on May 21, 1927, the life of Charles A. Lindbergh changed forever. He had just landed at Le Bourget airfield after a 33 1/2–hour flight from New York to Paris, becoming the first person to fly an airplane nonstop across the Atlantic Ocean. On the ground, he was confronted with 100,000 crazed and enthusiastic Frenchmen. The next day, the president of France presented him with the Legion of Honor. Medals from the kings of Belgium and England followed.

Upon Lindbergh's return to Washington, Pres. Calvin Coolidge presented him with the Distinguished Flying Cross and promoted him to the rank of colonel in the Army Reserves. New York City greeted him with the largest ticker tape parade in the city's history, attended by four million people. Here, he received the Medal of Valor. Lindbergh, the overwhelmed, shy, 25-year-old farm boy from the Midwest, had instantly become the first multimedia hero—the world's first superstar.

The flight marked the beginning of a new life for Lindbergh, one where the public and the press would constantly hound him. This was also the beginning of "Lindbergh mania." Two weeks after his flight, the US Postal Department issued a 10¢ airmail stamp with his plane, the *Spirit of St. Louis*, depicted on it. There were Lindbergh-themed banks, songs, bookends, calendars, jewelry, tapestries, bed linens, cigars, dinnerware, pins, and good-luck pieces. The world went crazy for anything Lindbergh related!

Lindbergh soon made a nationwide tour to promote aviation. This took him to 92 cities in 48 states, where he delivered 147 speeches and rode 1,290 miles in parades. In December 1927, he embarked on a 9,000-mile aviation tour of Latin America countries. While spending Christmas in Mexico with the American ambassador, Dwight Morrow, he met his future wife, Anne Morrow.

When Lindbergh returned to the United States, President Coolidge presented him with the Congressional Medal of Honor, and his plane was retired to the Smithsonian Institution. Lindbergh was exhausted and longed for peace and quiet. After he married, he needed to find someplace to live, far away from the public and press.

Charles Lindbergh electrified the world. At only 25 years old, he would attempt to do what many men had already failed to do—fly nonstop across the Atlantic Ocean. Wanting to win a $25,000 prize offered by hotel owner Raymond Orteig, Lindbergh, defying all odds, designed and built a single-engine monoplane that he named the *Spirit of St. Louis*. (Courtesy of James G. Davidson.)

The Ryan Aircraft Company in San Diego, California, built the *Spirit of St. Louis*. Charles Lindbergh helped design the aircraft and lived in the hangar while supervising its construction. He began referring to himself and his plane as "we." When he returned from home, he wrote about the flight in a book titled *We* that was republished in 1953 as the Pulitzer Prize–winning *The Spirit of St. Louis*. (Courtesy of James G. Davidson.)

Even before his flight, Charles Lindbergh had acquired many nicknames, including "Slim" and "Plucky." After his flight, "Lucky Lindy" was added. In May 1927, Lindbergh flew from San Diego to St. Louis, where he showed his investors his plane, and then he flew on to Roosevelt Field on Long Island. (Courtesy of James G. Davidson.)

"PLUCKY" LINDBERGH
Ready to "Hop Off"

Capt. Charles "Plucky" Lindbergh
Ready to Take Off on His
New York to Paris Flight, May 20, 1927

There were several pilots on Long Island who hoped to take off at the same time as Charles Lindbergh. All of the competitors' planes had multiple engines and a crew except for Lindbergh, who chose a single-engine plane and no crew. Daily, crowds came to the airport to see who might be taking off on this epic flight. Because of foul weather, it appeared everyone would be grounded for some time. (Courtesy of James G. Davidson.)

11

The
"SPIRIT OF ST. LOUIS"
Puts out to Sea

Sensing a break in the weather, Charles Lindbergh chanced an early-morning flight on May 20, 1927. At 7:52 a.m., overloaded with gas and with a crowd of 500 watching, the *Spirit of St. Louis* took off, barely clearing the telephone wires at the end of the runway. Lindbergh landed in Paris at 10:22 p.m. on May 21, where 100,000 people at the airfield rushed his plane. (Courtesy of James G. Davidson.)

OUR HERO
CHAS. A. LINDBERGH

NEW YORK   PARIS

MAY 21, 1927

Charles Lindbergh was awarded the Legion of Honor by the French president, followed by medals from King Albert I of Belgium and King George V of England. But America wanted "the Lone Eagle" back home to celebrate his achievement. Therefore, Pres. Calvin Coolidge sent the cruiser USS *Memphis* to Cherbourg, France, to pick up Lindbergh and his plane and bring them back to Washington, DC. (Courtesy of James G. Davidson.)

A majestic convoy of warships and aircraft escorted Charles Lindbergh into Washington. He received the first Distinguished Flying Cross ever awarded from President Coolidge on June 11 in a ceremony at the Washington Monument where he was also made a colonel in the Army Reserves. The ceremony was broadcast live on the radio, the first of its kind. (Courtesy of the New Jersey State Police Museum.)

A blizzard of ticker tape greeted Charles Lindbergh on his return to New York City. Lower Broadway turned white in a shower of ticker tape and confetti that floated down from every window along the route of his welcoming parade. Spectators lined the parade route, leaned out of windows, and even sat on the rooftops in an attempt to catch a glimpse of their hero. (Courtesy of James G. Davidson.)

Charles Lindbergh's reception into New York City was the wildest in the city's history, as four million people lined his parade route for the largest ticker tape parade ever. Mayor Jimmy Walker pinned New York's Medal of Valor on him. Here is a program from that night's Mayor's Reception for Lindbergh at the Hotel Commodore. (Courtesy of James G. Davidson.)

Charles Lindbergh's epic flight would become the one singular event that would electrify the world and change transportation forever. To honor him, the US Postal Service issued this 10¢ airmail stamp, depicting the *Spirit of St. Louis*, on June 13, 1927, the very day Lindbergh returned to Washington. (Courtesy of James G. Davidson.)

Raymond Orteig was a French-born New York hotel owner. In 1919, he had lunch with Eddie Rickenbacker, the famous World War I ace. Impressed by the possibilities of aviation, Orteig offered a $25,000 prize for the first successful nonstop flight between New York and Paris. In 1927, when Charles Lindbergh beat the odds, he received the prize money personally from Orteig upon his return to New York. (Courtesy of James G. Davidson.)

As soon as Charles Lindbergh landed, everything became Lindbergh-themed. Over 200 songs were written about him, including "Lindy with the Heart of Gold," "We," "Lindbergh, the Eagle of the USA," "Lindy Did It," "The Spirit of St. Louis March," and at left, "Lucky Lindy." The Lindy hop, which he never danced to, was also inspired by him. (Courtesy of James G. Davidson.)

IMPROVED EDITION

Lindy

The New
FLYING GAME

A Sequel to the
Famous Parker Game TOURING

Parker Brothers Inc
SALEM, MASS., NEW YORK, LONDON

LUCKY LINDY
PARFUM
NIPOLA CO
ST. PAUL

Just about everything anyone could imagine was reproduced with a Charles Lindbergh theme. It was now possible to purchase calendars, banks, bookends, tapestries, sheets and pillowcases, silverware and dishes, all with the likeness of Lindbergh or the *Spirit of St. Louis* on them. The famous Parker Brothers Company issued an "improved edition" of Lindy: The New Flying Game. (Courtesy of James G. Davidson.)

Toy stores and novelty shops around the country carried an endless series of Charles Lindbergh-themed jigsaw puzzles; jewelry and jewelry boxes; pens, pencils, and pencil cases; penknives; and poker chips. The Nipola Products Company of St. Paul, Minnesota, even made Lucky Lindy perfumes. Allegedly, this was used as a front for bootleggers during Prohibition! (Courtesy of James G. Davidson.)

A frenzy of merchandising quickly ensued after the flight. Watch fobs were decorative medallions attached to a pocket watch by a chain. This photograph shows just a few of the watch fobs that were available at the time, all with a Charles Lindbergh theme. Notice the fob with the compass. (Courtesy of James G. Davidson.)

Many schoolchildren had a soft pilot's helmet like "Lindy's" that they would wear to school. The hobby of collecting Charles Lindbergh pin backs, such as those shown in this photograph, became the latest fad. The Bond Bread company (now the General Host Corporation) issued a series of aviation-themed pins, with Lindbergh and the *Spirit of St. Louis* as pin No. 1. (Courtesy of James G. Davidson.)

Upon his return from Paris, Charles Lindbergh was talked into a three-month nationwide tour to promote aviation. During that trip, he touched down in all 48 states, visited 92 cities, and gave 147 speeches. The Lindbergh frenzy was unending. Each stop sponsored special postal cachets,

like the ones shown below. It was common to have 50,000 to 100,000 people turn out to see him at these events. It was estimated that 30 million Americans saw him within the first six months of his return to America. (All, courtesy of James G. Davidson.)

Various societies issued Lindbergh commemorative medals. Just about everyone owned a "Lindbergh Lucky Coin" of some sort. These were either commemorative coins, like those shown at left, or advertisements of some sort. However, President Coolidge gave Charles Lindbergh's most prestigious medal to him. On March 21, 1929, he was presented with the Congressional Medal of Honor at a ceremony in which he turned his plane, the *Spirit of St. Louis*, over to the Smithsonian Institution. Pictured below is a commemorative postcard that was printed to commemorate Lindbergh's visit to Milwaukee in August 1927. It depicts just how crowded any event Lindbergh attended could be. (Both, courtesy of James G. Davidson.)

Returning to New York exhausted, Lindbergh was asked by Dwight Morrow, the American ambassador to Mexico, to repeat his aviation promotional tour in South America. He flew to Mexico City in December 1927 and ultimately on to 28 countries and islands. Ambassador Morrow asked Lindbergh and his mother to spend the Christmas holidays in Mexico City with his family. It was here that he met Anne Morrow, a senior at Smith College. (Courtesy of James G. Davidson.)

Erratically corresponding by letter, Charles Lindbergh had his first date with Anne Morrow in the spring of 1929. It was the first date he had ever had. Two weeks later, he asked Anne to marry him. They were married on May 27, 1929, at the Morrow estate in Englewood, New Jersey. (Courtesy of James G. Davidson.)

Charles and Anne Lindbergh wished to build their new home as far from the press and public as possible. During the summer of 1930, they purchased 425 acres on the Sourland Mountains in East Amwell, New Jersey, not far from Princeton. Because of the property's proximity to the village of Hopewell, the Lindberghs referred to their new home as the Hopewell House. It would not receive its more famous name of Highfields until 1933. There was a brook and small wooded area of old oak trees, but the majority of the property—like most of the Sourland Mountains—was open fields. Secluded and far from any major city, Colonel Lindbergh planned to add an airstrip on his property so he could fly rather than drive to New York, Boston, or elsewhere. During the construction of the house, the Lindberghs rented a farmhouse on Cold Soil Road in nearby Lawrence Township called White Cloud Farm. (Courtesy of James G. Davidson.)

Chester Aldrich, the architect who designed the Morrow estate in Englewood, New Jersey, was hired to design the Lindberghs' new house. The Matthews Construction Company of Princeton supplied the majority of laborers for the project. The house is a two-and-a-half-story stone structure of mixed architectural style—French Revival and English Tudor Revival. There are 23 rooms, six fireplaces, and 34 closets in the house. The house is built like a fortress, with reinforced concrete floors and stone walls that are 28 inches thick. The exterior walls have a white stucco finish, and the steep gabled slate roof was designed to resemble the ripples of the Atlantic Ocean when seen from the air. The privacy the Lindberghs desired was short lived. Shortly after the quarter-mile-long driveway was completed in March 1931, the foundations were dug and sightseers arrived. (Courtesy of James G. Davidson.)

Charles Augustus Lindbergh Jr., the first of the Lindbergh's six children, was born on June 22, 1930. The media circus continued. The baby was featured on the cover of magazine and even had a song written about him. He became affectionately known as "the Eaglet." (Courtesy of James G. Davidson.)

Charles Lindbergh Jr. celebrated his first birthday party at Next Day Hill, the Morrow estate in northern New Jersey, where Anne and Charles often stayed. On Halloween weekend 1931, the Lindberghs spent their first night at Highfields. The house was not completely finished, but it was their first home. (Courtesy of the New Jersey State Police Museum.)

Two

THE CRIME

The Lindberghs spent their first weekend at Highfields in October 1931. Because construction on the house was only partially completed, they only visited on the weekends. The routine was to travel to Hopewell on Friday or Saturday and return to Next Day Hill, the Morrow estate in Englewood, on Sunday or Monday. During their stay at Highfields over the last weekend in February 1932, both Anne and Charles Jr. had colds, so they altered their routine for the first time. They stayed an additional two nights, with plans to leave on Wednesday.

Tuesday, March 1, was a cold, damp, dreary day. Because she was feeling unwell, Anne asked Betty Gow, the baby's nanny, who had stayed behind in Englewood, to come to Hopewell to help care for the baby. That night, at 7:00 p.m., Betty and Anne put little Charlie to bed, first rubbing his chest with Vicks Vapo Rub. Betty quickly stitched an undershirt that was worn under his Dr. Denton's sleeping suit, and metal thumb guards were put on him to keep him from sucking his thumb. He was then put to bed, with the sheets pinned to the mattress.

Charles Lindbergh returned from Manhattan at 8:20 p.m. At 9:30 p.m., after eating dinner, Anne went upstairs to take a bath, and Lindbergh sat in the library, directly under the nursery. At 10:00 p.m., Betty checked on the baby and discovered he was not in his crib. After checking with the Lindberghs, who did not have the baby, they realized he had been kidnapped. They searched in and around the house, and the Hopewell and New Jersey State Police were called. Roadblocks were quickly set up and all of the bridges and tunnels going in and out of the state were secured.

Lindbergh assumed the lead role in the investigation. His first concern was getting his son back, not arresting the kidnappers. A note on the windowsill in the baby's nursery demanded a $50,000 ransom. Strangely, when the room was dusted for fingerprints, none, not even those of the family, were to be found.

Colonel Lindbergh quickly realized his missing son must have been kidnapped. Upon calling the Hopewell and New Jersey State Police, Lindbergh began searching the house and grounds around his home with a flashlight. Soon, car lights and torches were used. People living in the area said that the Lindbergh house could be seen from miles away; it was lit up like a Christmas tree. (Courtesy of James G. Davidson.)

A teletype message was sent out from State Police Headquarters at 10:46 p.m. By 11:00 p.m., all bridges, roads, and tunnels in and around New Jersey were sealed and roadblocks were set up throughout the tristate area. By 11:15 p.m., the first reporter, Edmund DeLong of the *New York Sun*, arrived at the estate. (Courtesy of the New Jersey State Police Museum.)

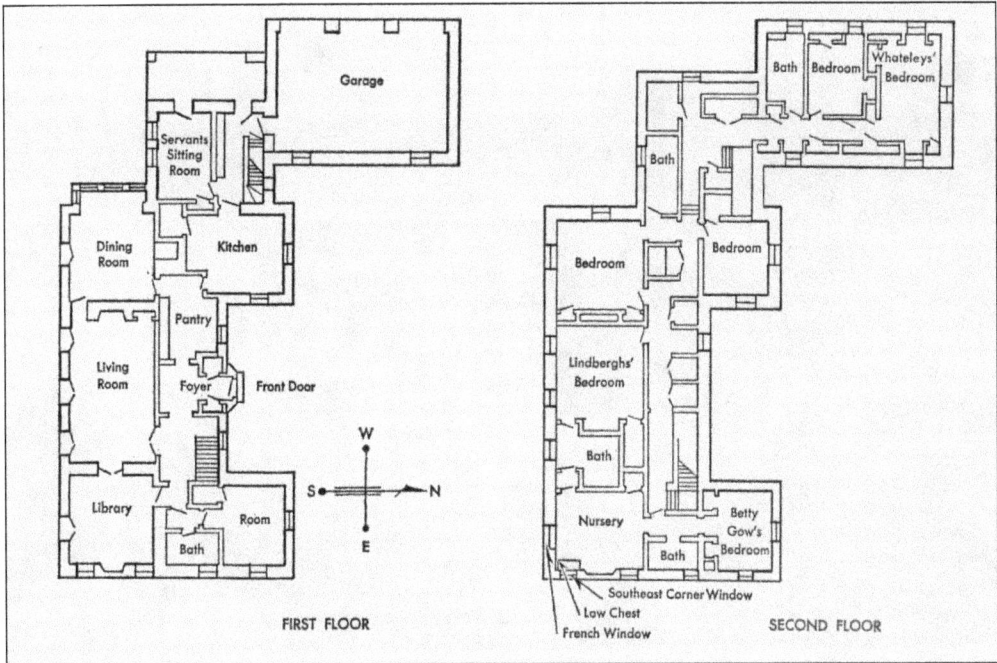

FIRST FLOOR   SECOND FLOOR

Charles Lindbergh had arrived home at 8:20 p.m. At approximately 9:00 p.m., after he and Anne finished their dinner, they went from the dining room to the living room, where he thought he heard a noise, which he attributed to something dropping in the kitchen, such as a wooden box. (Courtesy of the *Dial Press*.)

To commit the crime, the kidnapper would have had to climb up a ladder that ended 30 inches below the window. He would have to open the shutters and window and climb through. Once inside, he had to clear a small cabinet that had a suitcase on it next to the window and then walk across the small room, dodging a table and screen that protected the crib from drafts. (Courtesy of the New Jersey State Police Museum.)

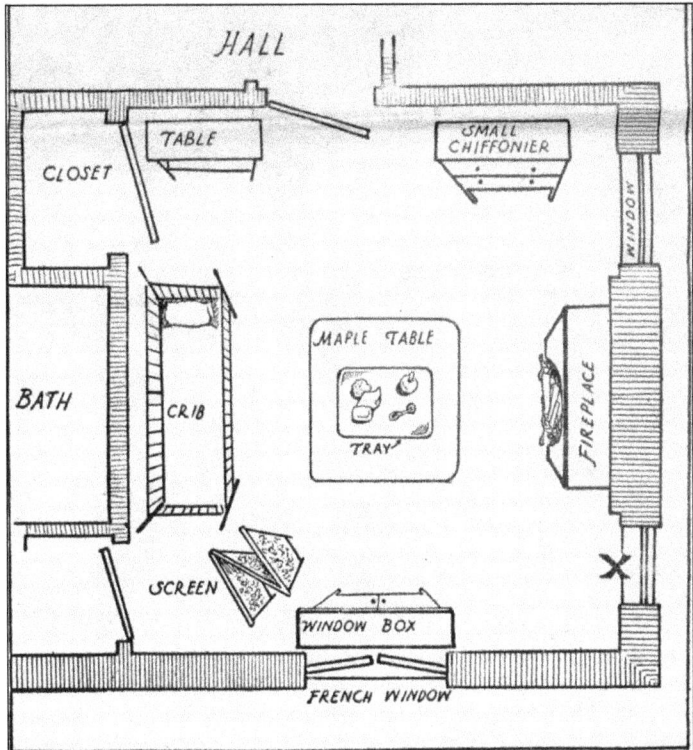

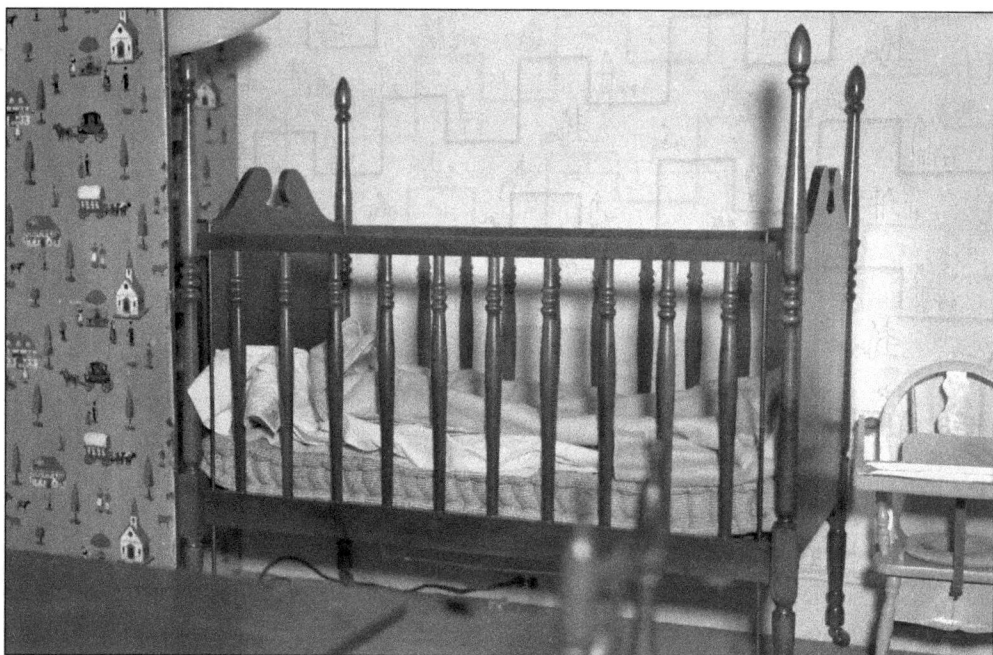

Charlie's blankets were pinned to the mattress with two large safety pins near his head. These were still in place after the kidnapping, which suggested to police that the baby had been yanked out of the crib by his feet. With no odor of chloroform in the room, investigators wondered why the baby did not cry. (Courtesy of the New Jersey State Police Museum.)

The kidnapper of the Lindbergh baby entered the nursery though this window on the southeast corner of the house. The kidnapper left behind muddy footprints on the windowsill and the suitcase. The windowsills are at least a foot deep inside the house, and they serve as the vents for the forced-air heating system. (Courtesy of the New Jersey State Police Museum.)

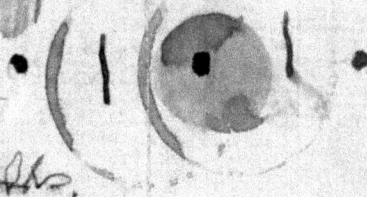

A ransom note demanding $50,000 was found on the windowsill. The note reads: "Dear Sir! Have 50.000 $ redy 25 000 $ in 20 $ bills 1.5000 $ in 10 $ bills and 10000 $ in 5 $ bills. After 2-4 days we will inform you where to deliver the money. We warn you for making anyding public or for notify the Police the chld is in gute care. Indication for all letters are singnature and 3 hohls." Because of its crudeness, misspellings and grammatical errors, the New Jersey State Police investigators believed that a foreigner who was not fluent in English, most likely someone from Germany, wrote the note. In addition to obviously disguised handwriting, one of the key features of the note was the "singnature" of a red dot, two blue interlocking rings, and three holes. This was to be the signature used on future communications from the kidnappers. There would be a total of 15 ransom notes, some of which were two-sided, received from the kidnappers over the next several weeks. (Courtesy of the New Jersey State Police Museum.)

The New York Times — LATE CITY EDITION

LINDBERGH BABY KIDNAPPED FROM HOME OF PARENTS ON FARM NEAR PRINCETON; TAKEN FROM HIS CRIB; WIDE SEARCH ON

The kidnapping of the world's most famous baby, Charles Lindbergh Jr., was front-page news the world over. Reporters immediately swarmed Highfields, the Lindbergh estate. By the next morning, 400 reporters had arrived in Hopewell. In just two days, the number had grown to 900. Because the estate was so large and unprotected, reporters and curiosity seekers initially were able to simply walk through the woods and contaminate the crime scene. The New Jersey State Police, Hopewell Police, and investigators from other police agencies in New Jersey were quickly on the scene. The eyes of the entire world were now focused on the tiny village of Hopewell, New Jersey. (Above, courtesy of James G. Davidson; below, courtesy of the New Jersey State Police Museum.)

The police determined through ladder prints in the mud under the window and scuff marks on the wall that only two sections of the three-section homemade extension ladder had been used. Two of the ladder rails had cracked and may have been the sound Colonel Lindbergh heard. It was speculated at the time that it broke under the extra weight of the kidnapper carrying the baby down the ladder. (Courtesy of the New Jersey State Police Museum.)

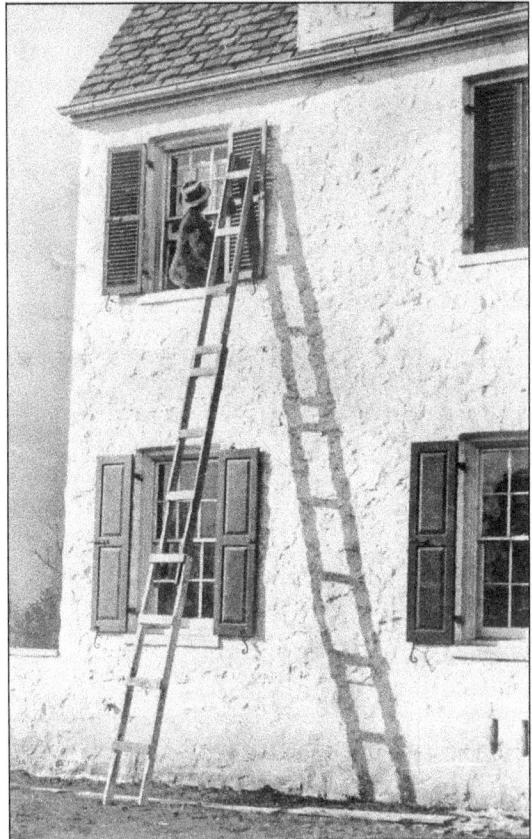

The New Jersey State Police attempted to accurately reenact the crime. Eventually it was determined that while the two-section ladder was too short to reach the window, three sections were too long, making it impossible to open the shutters all the way. Some investigators began to suspect the kidnapping was an inside job and the baby was simply handed out the window to an accomplice. (Courtesy of the New Jersey State Police Museum.)

At about 4:00 a.m. the following morning, the New Jersey State Police and Charles Lindbergh employed a local tracker, Oscar Bush, to follow footprints found near the crime scene. He followed what appeared to be two sets of footprints through a field to Featherbed Lane, where he speculated that a getaway car had been waiting. (Courtesy of the Historical Society of Princeton.)

Every good murder mystery has an English butler, and Olly Whateley was Lindbergh's. Born in England, Olly and his wife, Elsie, were hired by Charles Lindbergh on October 15, 1930. Olly's duties were that of a butler and general handyman. During the week, while the Lindberghs were in Englewood, Olly would often show strangers through the house to break the boredom. He died from a stomach ailment in 1933. (Courtesy of the New Jersey State Police Museum.)

Elsie Whateley served as the Lindberghs' housekeeper and cook. She and her husband, Olly, immigrated to the United States in March 1930. After her husband's death, Elsie continued to work for the Lindberghs. Suffering from cancer, she returned to England in late 1935 and died on January 8, 1936. (Courtesy of the New Jersey State Police Museum.)

Betty Gow had been employed as the Lindberghs' nanny for a little over a year. Born in Glasgow, Scotland, she immigrated three years earlier and was very dedicated to taking care of little Charlie. When the state police and the FBI strongly suggested to Charles Lindbergh that the kidnapping might have been an inside job, he refused to allow the police to interrogate his staff beyond general questions. (Courtesy of the Jersey City Free Public Library.)

One of the (many) mysteries of the Lindbergh Case was that of the Lindberghs' dog, Wahgoosh. A fox terrier, Wahgoosh was known to bark at everything, but on the night of the kidnapping, the dog never barked. This added fuel to the speculation that the crime must have been an inside job. (Courtesy of the New Jersey State Police Museum.)

To All Law Enforcement Officials, Wardens of Penal Institutions, Etc.

Reproduced below will be found specimens of the handwriting represented by two notes transmitted by the alleged kidnapers in the Lindbergh case:

It is requested that you search the records containing the handwriting of all prisoners in your custody, or any persons coming under your observation or cognizance, for the purpose of ascertaining whether any of the specimens of said handwriting are similar to those indicated above. Should you have reasonable grounds to suspect that any of the handwriting which you may observe is similar to that of the specimen forwarded, it would be appreciated if you would, at the earliest possible moment, transmit specimens thereof, together with all available data relative to the individuals whose handwriting is forwarded, to—

COLONEL H. NORMAN SCHWARZKOPF,

May 21, 1932. Superintendent of State Police, Trenton, New Jersey.

Posters with photographs of excerpts from the ransom notes were sent to law enforcement agencies and prisons around the country. Officials were requested to compare the handwriting found in the ransom notes to that of prisoners in their institutions. Should a similar specimen be found, it was to be forwarded to Col. H. Norman Schwarzkopf of the New Jersey State Police. (Courtesy of the New Jersey State Police Museum.)

34

Wanted posters requesting information as to the whereabouts of Charles Lindbergh Jr. were distributed all over the United States and around the world, as evidenced by this one from Mexico. The New Jersey State Police, local police departments, the Bureau of Investigation (later known as the FBI), the Army Air Corps, the Postal Inspection Service, and the Coast Guard were all put at Lindbergh's disposal. Within 24 hours of the kidnapping, 100,000 people—police officers and citizens—were looking for the Lindbergh baby in a nationwide manhunt. A misprint on the poster led to some confusion over the size of the baby. It should have read 2 feet 9 inches, not 29 inches. (Right, courtesy of the New Jersey State Police Museum; below, courtesy of James G. Davidson.)

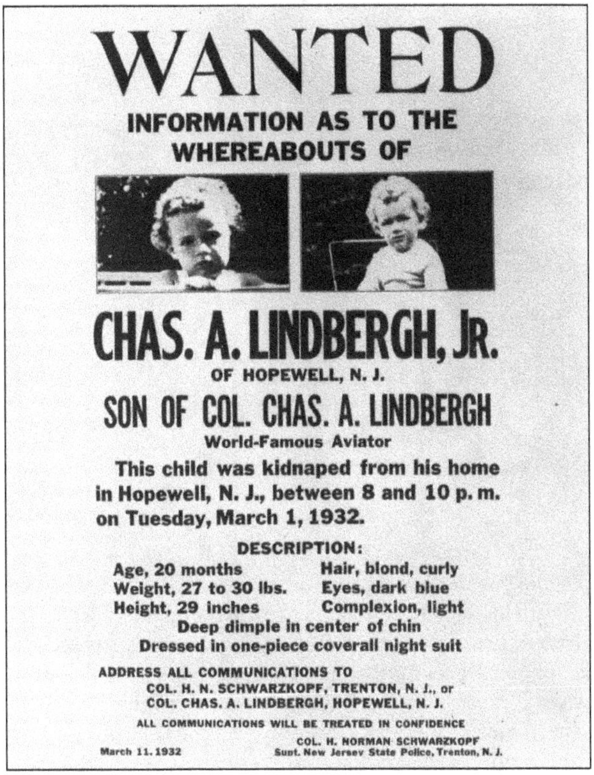

WANTED

INFORMATION AS TO THE WHEREABOUTS OF

CHAS. A. LINDBERGH, JR.

OF HOPEWELL, N. J.

SON OF COL. CHAS. A. LINDBERGH
World-Famous Aviator

This child was kidnaped from his home in Hopewell, N. J., between 8 and 10 p. m. on Tuesday, March 1, 1932.

DESCRIPTION:

Age, 20 months	Hair, blond, curly
Weight, 27 to 30 lbs.	Eyes, dark blue
Height, 29 inches	Complexion, light
Deep dimple in center of chin	
Dressed in one-piece coverall night suit	

ADDRESS ALL COMMUNICATIONS TO
COL. H. N. SCHWARZKOPF, TRENTON, N. J., or
COL. CHAS. A. LINDBERGH, HOPEWELL, N. J.

ALL COMMUNICATIONS WILL BE TREATED IN CONFIDENCE

March 11. 1932

COL. H. NORMAN SCHWARZKOPF
Supt. New Jersey State Police, Trenton, N. J.

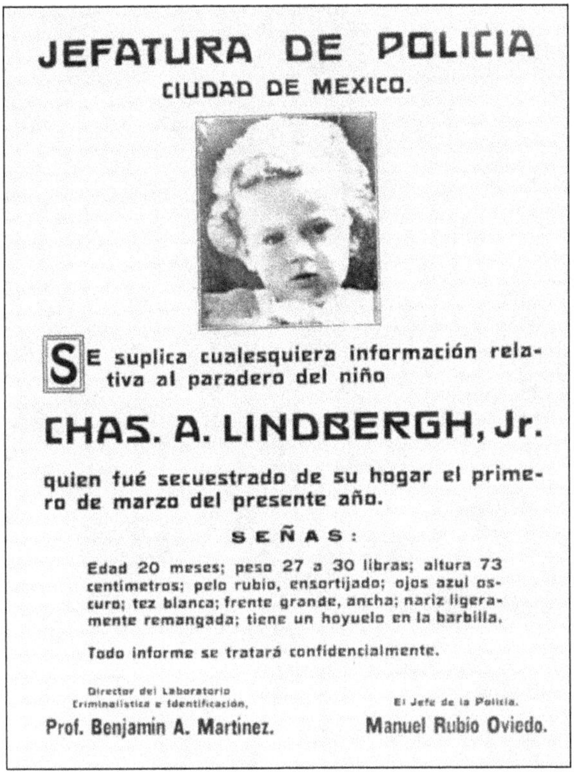

JEFATURA DE POLICIA
CIUDAD DE MEXICO.

SE suplica cualesquiera información relativa al paradero del niño

CHAS. A. LINDBERGH, Jr.

quien fué secuestrado de su hogar el primero de marzo del presente año.

SEÑAS:

Edad 20 meses; peso 27 a 30 libras; altura 73 centímetros; pelo rubio, ensortijado; ojos azul oscuro; tez blanca; frente grande, ancha; nariz ligeramente remangada; tiene un hoyuelo en la barbilla.

Todo informe se tratará confidencialmente.

Director del Laboratorio
Criminalística e Identificación,

Prof. Benjamin A. Martinez.

El Jefe de la Policía.

Manuel Rubio Oviedo.

Highfields was in East Amwell Township, New Jersey, but the closest town was Hopewell, about three miles away. The Lindberghs frequently visited the small, sleepy town. When news of the kidnapping became known, Hopewell quickly filled with reporters and photographers. Gebhart's was a luncheonette on Broad Street owned by Paul Gebhart that also had rooms to rent. It soon served meals 24 hours a day and became the spot for reporters to pick up the latest tips about the Lindbergh Case. (Both, courtesy of the Hopewell Museum.)

Almost as quickly as the reporters arrived, the Army Signal Corps laid a communications cable overland from Trenton, across farmers' fields, to the Reading Railroad station in Hopewell. The station became the communications hub for reporters, housing teletype machines and banks of telephones. The Town of Hopewell had to hire an additional 20 telephone operators to man the new telephone lines. (Courtesy of the Hopewell Historical Society.)

Cars of reporters and sightseers clogged the roads near the Lindbergh estate, while hundreds of other people walked through the woods to the house. Finally, the New Jersey State Police set up a perimeter around the 425-acre property. Here, Charles Cavalier, a representative of the police, is telling the reporters that they will have to leave the property. Reporters were to be kept two miles from the estate. (Courtesy of the Jersey City Free Public Library.)

Being kicked off the estate did not deter the determined press. One news agency rented two ambulances that it periodically pressed into service if it thought it could get a scoop ahead of its competitors. Others, as seen here, climbed trees in hopes of catching a glimpse of something—anything—that they could use in their tabloids. (Courtesy of the Jersey City Free Public Library.)

Because Charles Lindbergh Jr. was able to say a few words, these toys from his nursery were given to John F. Condon, a teacher who offered to be an intermediary with the kidnappers, to show to the baby to see if he could name them. This, it was believed, would help to assure Condon that it was the Lindbergh baby and that he was in fact dealing with the actual kidnappers. (Courtesy of the New Jersey State Police Museum.)

Three

THE SEARCH

By the morning of March 2, 1932, the Sourland Mountains and Hopewell, New Jersey, were flooded with reporters, photographers, police, and curious sightseers. The entire area around Highfields was searched. A week after the kidnapping, a semiretired teacher in the Bronx, Dr. John F. Condon, wrote a letter to the editor of the *Bronx Home News* offering suggestions for the return of the child. Allegedly, the editor added that Condon would willingly serve as an intermediary as well. Amazingly, the kidnappers contacted him, and negotiations ensued.

Dr. Condon met with one of the kidnappers, nicknamed "Cemetery John" by the press, in Woodlawn Cemetery in the Bronx on March 12. Condon refused to pay the ransom until he had further proof that he was dealing with the actual kidnappers. Several days later, he received a Dr. Denton's sleeping suit believed to belong to the Lindbergh baby. Convinced that he was indeed in touch with the kidnappers, Dr. Condon met again with Cemetery John on April 2. This time, he handed over $50,000 in gold certificates in return for a note stating that the baby could be found on a boat called *Nellie* off the coast of Martha's Vineyard. The next day, Colonel Lindbergh began to search for his son.

Police investigated all possible leads, including the mafia, local criminals, and both the Lindbergh and Morrow household staff. Every worker who had ever worked on the construction of Highfields was questioned, as were many locals.

On May 12, two local workmen were driving their truck along the Hopewell-Princeton Road when one of them, William Allen, needed to answer the call of nature. They pulled over, and as Allen walked into the woods, he discovered the corpse of a baby lying face down in a shallow grave. The police were called, and they took the corpse to the morgue in Trenton. Betty Gow, the baby's nanny, and Colonel Lindbergh both identified the corpse as that of Charles Lindbergh Jr. After an autopsy was performed, Lindbergh ordered the baby's remains cremated. With the baby now dead, the kidnapping case turned into a murder investigation.

Col. H. Norman Schwarzkopf was the superintendent of the New Jersey State Police. He was a graduate of West Point and a veteran of the First World War. When the state police was established in 1921, the 25-year-old Schwarzkopf was appointed as its first superintendent. The Lindbergh kidnapping was the first major investigation conducted by the young organization. Therefore, Schwarzkopf accepted the assistance of more experienced detectives from both the Jersey City Police Department and the Newark Police Department. However, he confessed to the *New York Evening Journal* in 1935 that he had turned over control to Charles Lindbergh. All aspects of the investigation first had to be cleared personally by Lindbergh. "I admit that there wasn't one single important step taken by us until we consulted Colonel Lindbergh to learn if we would be interfering with his chances of getting back the baby." That changed, however, when the baby was found dead on May 12, 1932. (Courtesy of the New Jersey State Police Museum.)

New York American EXTRA

CHARACTER QUALITY · AMERICA FIRST! · ENTERPRISE

AN AMERICAN PAPER FOR THE AMERICAN PEOPLE

THURSDAY, MARCH 3, 1932—36 PAGES

Lindbergh Confident Kidnaped Baby Will Be Home by Noon; Ready to Pay $50,000 Ransom Asked by Abductors

Early on, the press knew that the kidnappers demanded a $50,000 ransom. During the Great Depression, kidnapping, especially of wealthy individuals, was quite common. Charles Lindbergh felt that the kidnapping of his son was a professional job, probably carried out by the New York mob. He felt reasonably sure that once he had paid the ransom, his son would be safely returned. (Courtesy of the New Jersey State Police Museum.)

The New Jersey State Police set up a temporary headquarters in the Lindberghs' three-car garage. Twenty telephone lines were installed and teletype machines were brought in to communicate with State Police Headquarters in Trenton. The Lindberghs' living and dining rooms were outfitted with mattresses for the police to sleep on, and meals for 40 people were sent from the Morrow estate in Englewood, New Jersey, three times a day. (Courtesy of the New Jersey State Police Museum.)

The New Jersey State Police eventually took over an abandoned house at the end of the Lindberghs' driveway. It was used as a barracks for the troopers assigned to Highfields, and a gate was installed. From this vantage point, the state police could monitor everyone who came in and out of the estate. Every car that passed by the driveway was stopped, the occupants questioned, and their license plate number written down. This practice continued until after the trial, three years later. (Courtesy of the New Jersey State Police Museum.)

The day after the kidnapping, March 2, police investigators and photographers searched the estate looking for and photographing evidence and clues. In addition to the three-section ladder, the police found a 3/4-inch Buck Bros. chisel and footprints leading to nearby Featherbed Lane. Ladder marks in the mud also aided the police in discerning that only two sections of the ladder were used in the execution of the crime. (Courtesy of the New Jersey State Police Museum.)

In just a few days, over 500 buildings had been searched within a three-mile radius of the Lindbergh estate. Every house, barn, shed, and shack was investigated. Many houses had been abandoned due to the Depression. Nearby, a shantytown-type camp was thoroughly searched. Within a week, the search radius was extended to five miles. (Courtesy of the New Jersey State Police Museum.)

Every well in the area had its pump pulled and the well hole searched. Residents became furious when they had to put their property back together themselves. Because the area was rural, the police found families living so deep in the woods that they had not heard of the kidnapping even a week after it had occurred. (Courtesy of the New Jersey State Police Museum.)

New Jersey governor A. Harry Moore (center) immediately contacted Charles Lindbergh and offered a $25,000 reward for the apprehension of the kidnappers. Lindbergh asked him to rescind the offer, as it might hinder his own negotiations with the kidnappers through John Condon. When the baby was found dead, Governor Moore again offered the reward. (Courtesy of the New Jersey State Police Museum.)

Within a few days of the kidnapping, Gov. A. Harry Moore called a conference of more than a dozen major city police organizations, police chiefs, detectives, and federal agencies. They met at the state house in Trenton on March 5, 1932, to develop a unified plan of action that would link federal, state, county, and municipal agencies in the investigation. (Courtesy of Mark W. Falzini.)

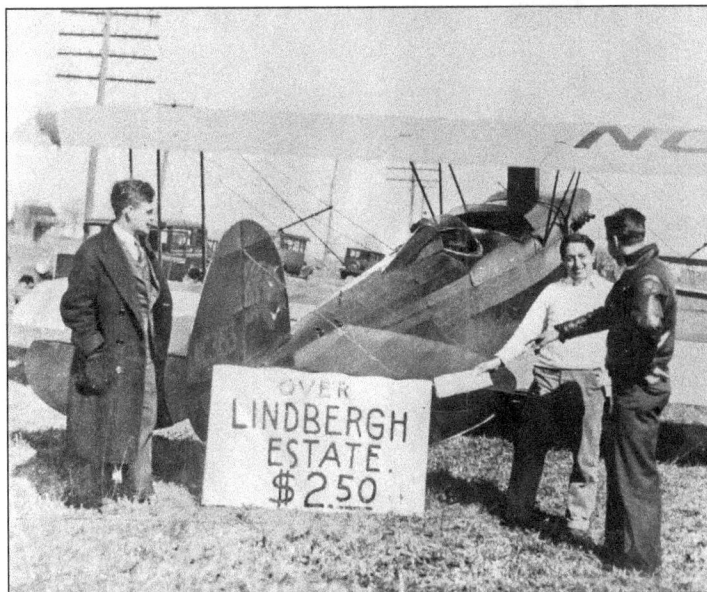

The day after the kidnapping, a temporary airstrip was set up east of Hopewell. Friends of Lindbergh who belonged to a flying fraternity, the Quiet Birdmen, flew in and took state police photographers over the Sourland Mountains to photograph the landscape and look for clues. Before long, barnstormers arrived and gave rides over the estate to the curious— for a small fee. (Courtesy of the New Jersey State Police Museum.)

45

Just outside Hopewell was St. Michael's Orphanage. The orphanage had 306 children living there at the time of the kidnapping, and it was speculated by some that the corpse found in the woods nearby could have been a missing orphan rather than the Lindbergh baby. Elmira Dormer, who ran the orphanage, testified at the Hauptmann trial that there were no children missing from the orphanage. (Courtesy of the Hopewell Historical Society.)

Trying to drum up any news or excitement about the case, the press became relentless in fabricating stories. Often, they would stage photographs, but the captions would read as if the action captured was spontaneous. Here, they had orphans at St. Michael's Orphanage pose as if saying prayers for the safe return of the Lindbergh baby. (Courtesy of the Jersey City Free Public Library.)

The Lindberghs immediately began to receive thousands of letters from the public—40,000 in the first month alone! One quarter were sympathy letters, one quarter came from psychics or people who had dreams about the baby, one quarter offered suggestions for the investigation, and the rest were crank letters. The Hopewell mailman delivered sacks of mail to the Lindbergh estate four times a day. (Courtesy of the New Jersey State Police Museum.)

Dr. John F. "Jafsie" Condon was a 71-year-old semiretired teacher who lived in the Bronx. A man of great physical strength for his age, he had been a part-time college professor as well as an elementary school principal. He loved mathematical puzzles and was a frequent contributor of patriotic poems and essays to his local newspaper, the *Bronx Home News*. (Courtesy of the New Jersey State Police Museum.)

The eccentric John Condon was outraged by the kidnapping of the Lindbergh baby and wrote a letter to the *Bronx Home News* offering $1,000 of his own money in addition to the $50,000 Lindbergh was to pay. Shortly after the editorial appeared in the paper, he received an anonymous letter appointing him to act as the intermediary between the kidnappers and the Lindbergh family. (Courtesy of Richard Sloan.)

Often, John Condon could be found frequenting Rosenhain's Restaurant in the Bronx with his friend and former heavyweight boxer Al Reich. It was from here that Condon called Highfields to inform Charles Lindbergh that he had received an answer to his newspaper appeal. When Condon described a signature of interlocking rings, Lindbergh asked him to immediately come to Hopewell. Condon had actually received a note from the kidnappers! (Courtesy of the New Jersey State Police Museum.)

John Condon was instructed to place advertisements in the *New York American* newspaper that he signed with a code name, "Jafsie," to which the kidnappers would reply with a letter of instructions. One letter, hand-delivered to him by taxi driver Joseph Perrone, instructed Condon to meet with a member of the kidnap gang at Woodlawn Cemetery in the Bronx. (Courtesy of the New Jersey State Police Museum.)

John Condon met with a man, whom the press dubbed "Cemetery John," by the gates to Woodlawn Cemetery. Just as they were meeting for the first time, a cemetery guard approached, and Cemetery John fled across the street with Condon running after him. Condon caught up with him at nearby Van Cortland Park, where they supposedly talked for over an hour on a bench next to a shed. (Courtesy of the New Jersey State Police Museum.)

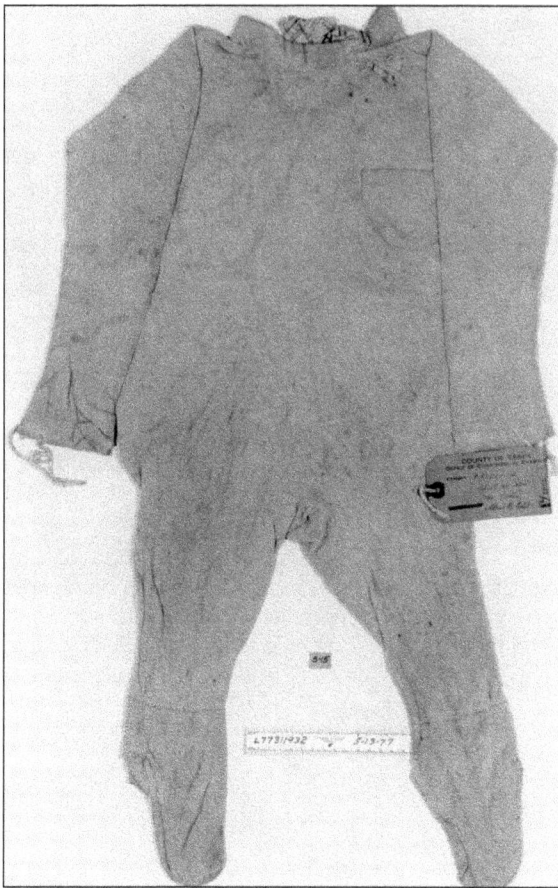

Cemetery John expected to receive the $50,000 ransom, but John Condon refused to pay until he was sure that Cemetery John actually had the Lindbergh baby. Condon asked to see the baby, but instead, the kidnapper mailed Condon this Dr. Denton's sleeping suit, which Charles Lindbergh tentatively identified as being similar to the one on the baby the night of the kidnapping. (Courtesy of the New Jersey State Police Museum.)

SPECIAL NOTICE   86

THANKS. THAT LITTLE PACKAGE YOU SENT ME WAS IMMEDIATELY DELIVERED AND ACCEPTED AS REAL ARTICLE. SEE MY POSITION. OVER 50 YEARS IN BUSINESS AND CAN I PAY WITHOUT SEEING GOODS? COMMON SENSE MAKES ME TRUST YOU. PLEASE UNDERSTAND MY POSITION.
JAFSIE.

Convinced that the sleeping suit was indeed that of the Lindbergh baby, John Condon placed this advertisement confirming to the kidnappers that it was genuine but also asking to see the baby. Meanwhile, Charles Lindbergh authorized Condon to pay the ransom. Because payment had been delayed, the ransom had been increased to $70,000. The kidnappers were now threatening to raise it again, to $100,000. (Courtesy of the New Jersey State Police Museum.)

John Condon continued to negotiate through the newspaper with the kidnappers. On April 2, 1932, Condon was instructed to go to the Bergen Greenhouse, a nursery across the street from St. Raymond's Cemetery in the Bronx. Driven there by Charles Lindbergh himself, Condon found another ransom note with instructions under a table in front of the nursery. (Courtesy of the New Jersey State Police Museum.)

While John Condon was looking for Cemetery John at the entrance to St. Raymond's Cemetery, shown here, both he and Charles Lindbergh heard a man shout, "Hey Doctor!" It was Cemetery John. Condon hurried across the street and followed Cemetery John into the cemetery, where Condon somehow convinced him to accept the original $50,000 instead of the $70,000. (Courtesy of the New Jersey State Police Museum.)

John Condon refused to hand over the ransom money unless he received a receipt for it in return. Cemetery John agreed and went off to get him his receipt while Condon returned to Lindbergh's car to retrieve the money. After informing Lindbergh that he had saved him $20,000, Condon returned to the cemetery, where he handed the money over the hedgerow to Cemetery John. (Courtesy of the New Jersey State Police Museum.)

the boy is on Boad Nelly
it is a small Boad 28 feet
long, two person are on the
Boad. the are innosent.
you will find the Boad between
Horseneck Beach and gay Head
near Elizabeth Island.

Once he had the ransom money, Cemetery John handed the above receipt to John Condon. The last of the ransom notes to be received, it stated that the baby could be found on the "Boad *Nelly*" near Martha's Vineyard. The next morning, Charles Lindbergh chartered a seaplane and began the futile search for his missing son. (Courtesy of the New Jersey State Police Museum.)

Desperate to find his son, Charles Lindbergh fell prey to hoaxers like John Hughes Curtis, pictured here. Curtis was a bankrupt shipbuilder from Norfolk, Virginia, who convinced Lindbergh that he was in contact with the actual kidnappers of his son. He eventually confessed to the hoax, but not before leading Lindbergh on a wild goose chase from Cape May, New Jersey, to the coast of Virginia. (Courtesy of the New Jersey State Police Museum.)

Charles Lindbergh followed John Hughes Curtis to Virginia, where they charted the yacht *Marcon*, shown below, in hopes of a rendezvous with the kidnappers. For nearly two months, Lindbergh searched in vain for his son. It was while with Curtis on another boat, the *Cachalot*, off the coast of Cape May, New Jersey, that Lindbergh received tragic news. (Courtesy of the Jersey City Free Public Library.)

On May 12, 1932, seventy-seven days after the kidnapping of Charles Lindbergh Jr., two local workers, William Allen and Orville Wilson, were returning to Hopewell along the Hopewell-Princeton Road with a load of timber in their truck. When they reached Mount Rose Hill, Allen had to answer the call of nature. They pulled their truck over at the only clear spot along the road in the area of Mount Rose, and Allen jumped out of the truck. He crossed the street and walked into the woods. He was about 60 feet from his truck when he saw a very badly decomposed corpse lying face down in a shallow depression. He called to Wilson, who joined him, and they both agreed that the corpse was that of a child. The location was just about five miles away from the Lindbergh house. (Left, courtesy of Richard Sloan; below, courtesy of the New Jersey State Police Museum.)

William Allen (right) and Orville Wilson (below) raced into Hopewell, where they found police chief Charles Williamson in the barbershop. Williamson called the New Jersey State Police, and the area in Mount Rose was quickly roped off. The baby's corpse was taken to the Swayze and Margerum Funeral Home, which served as a morgue, in Trenton. The police sent for Betty Gow, the baby's nanny, to come to the morgue and try to identify the badly decomposed remains. She did this by providing a detailed description of the T-shirt she had made for him the night of the kidnapping. Charles Lindbergh also identified the decomposed remains as those of his son. (Both, courtesy of the Jersey City Free Public Library.)

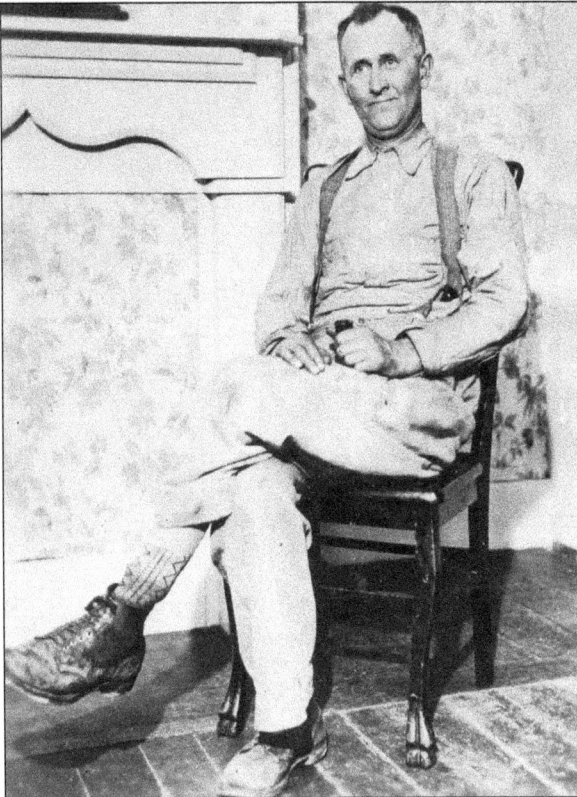

The location where the baby's remains were found became an immediate tourist attraction. The road was jammed with traffic for miles. One enterprising person opened a hot dog stand across the street from the gravesite. Meanwhile, Charles Lindbergh was out to sea off Cape May, New Jersey, with hoaxer John Hughes Curtis. When word reached him that his son's remains may have been found, he immediately returned to Trenton. (Above, courtesy of James G. Davidson; below, courtesy of the New Jersey State Police Museum.)

WALTER H. SWAYZE
TRENTON, NEW JERSEY

May 12, 1932

Report on Unknown baby

    Sex Undetermined due to marked decomposition of body.
    General appearence badly decomposed
    Left leg from knee down missing
    Left hand missing
    Right forearm missing
    Abdominal organs except liver missing
    Thoracic organs except heart missing
    Eyes softened & decomposed
    Skin of head ,face , portion of chest & right Foot
    discolored & decomposed
    Body shows evidence of prolpnged exposure & usual decomppositio
    that would occurin the course of approximately two to three
    months time depending on climatic and other conditions that
    might produce such results.
    Special charásteristics -
    Unusualy high & prominent forehead & cranium apparently
    greater in circumference than would be found in a child this
    age, The first toe of the right foot completely overlaps
    the large toe and the second toe of the right foot partialy ov
    overlaps the large toe,
    there are eight upper and eight lower teeth, the upper
    incisors are well formed rather prominent but do not protrude,
    the two lower canines tend to divert towardsand are below the
    line of the adjacent teeth.
    Height Thirty three and one half inches,light curly hair
    about three inches in length, and a section of skin on the
    right foot which had not become discolored indicated a child
    of the white race
    The facial muscles the only ones of the body that had not
    deteriorated would indicate a well developed child.
    Autopsy findings-.
    General decomposition of the muscle of the entire body
    and other soft tissues except the face, But marked
    discoloration and some disfigurement of this part of the body
    existed due to softening of the eyeballs and a swollen
    condition of the lips and tongue.
    there was also a fracture of the skull extending from the
    fontanel down the left side of the skull to a point posterior
    to the left ear where it bifurcatedinto two distinct fractures
    there was also a perforated fracture about a half inch in dia-
    meter on the right side of the skull posterior to the right
    ear, There was evidence of a hemorrhage on the inner surface
    of the left side of the skull at the point of fracture, the
    scalp was so badly decomposed that it was impossible to find
    any contusions or hemorrhagic external to the skull, The
    fontanel was not closed the opening in the skull at this point
    being about one inch in diameter.
    Diagnosis of the cause of death is a fractured skull due to
    external violence
                                        Signed

Once the corpse was at the morgue and a positive identification was made, an autopsy was performed by Mercer County physician Charles Mitchell. Because the corpse was so badly decomposed, it was impossible to determine its sex. The size of the corpse—2 feet 9 1/2 inches (or 33 1/2 inches)—matched that of the Lindbergh baby. The corpse also had light curly hair and overlapping toes, a feature the Lindbergh baby was known to have. The left leg, the left hand, and the right forearm were all missing. Of the internal organs, only the heart and liver remained. The cause of death was determined to have been a fractured skull due to external violence. Walter Swayze, who owned the funeral home and morgue, stated many years later that it was in fact he who had performed the autopsy under Dr. Mitchell's guidance. (Courtesy of the New Jersey State Police Museum.)

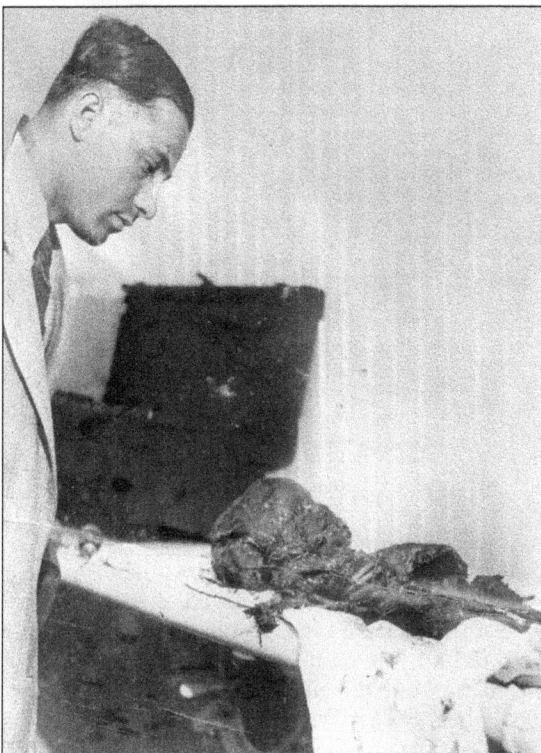

Dr. Charles H. Mitchell (above) began practicing medicine in New Jersey around 1900 and was the Mercer County physician since 1924. In addition to participating in the autopsy of the Lindbergh baby, Dr. Mitchell was also one of five medical attendants at the execution of Richard Hauptmann. While the autopsy was being performed at the morgue in Trenton, hundreds of people gathered outside the building. Somehow, a press photographer got into the morgue and took an unauthorized photograph of the corpse (at left) that appeared in many newspapers. Possibly because of this, Charles Lindbergh had his son's remains cremated the next day. (Both, courtesy of the New Jersey State Police Museum.)

Four

THE INVESTIGATION

The ransom, which consisted mostly of gold certificates, was paid on Saturday, April 2, 1932, and just two days later, some of those gold certificates began appearing in and around New York, especially Manhattan and the Bronx. The investigation, however, was not moving very fast. The New Jersey State Police and Colonel Schwarzkopf were receiving a lot of criticism for their failure to arrest a suspect. The FBI assisted the New York City Police with monitoring the appearance of ransom money. The New Jersey State Police and Jersey City Police detectives continued to investigate Morrow servants, especially Violet Sharp, who eventually committed suicide. Henry "Red" Johnson, the Norwegian boyfriend of Betty Gow, who was the first suspect to be arrested, was soon cleared of any involvement and returned home to Norway.

In 1933, in an attempt to bolster the economy during the Great Depression, the Roosevelt administration ordered the recall of all gold coins, gold bullion, and gold certificates from circulation. In September 1934, because it was no longer legal tender, a gas station attendant became suspicious when a customer paid for gas with a $10 gold certificate. He scribbled the license plate number of the car on the edge of the bill in case the bank did not accept it. When it was found to be ransom money, the police were called and, thanks to the license number, arrested Bruno Richard Hauptmann. After searching his house and garage, the police found a hidden cache of over $13,000 of the ransom money.

Getting Hauptmann to New Jersey to face trial required an extradition order. The authorities needed someone to identify Hauptmann as being at the scene of the crime. The lone potential eyewitness was a 17-year-old student, Ben Lupica, who lived near the Lindbergh estate. On the night of the kidnapping, he saw a man and a ladder in a dark sedan with New Jersey license plates. However, he could not identify Hauptmann.

With the lure of the $25,000 reward, two willing "eyewitnesses" came forward, and Richard Hauptmann was extradited to New Jersey to face trial for murder.

Initially, Col. H. Norman Schwarzkopf of the New Jersey State Police had acquiesced control of the investigation to Charles Lindbergh. Once the baby was found dead, Schwarzkopf took control of the murder investigation. It was believed that a gang perpetrated the crime with inside help. With ransom money turning up all over the New York area and no solid leads, Schwarzkopf took to the airwaves to appeal for information. (Courtesy of the New Jersey State Police Museum.)

Ben Lupica was a 17-year-old student who lived near Charles Lindbergh. On March 1, he was returning home from school when a dark sedan passed him on the wrong side of the road. In the car were a man and a ladder. Lupica said that the car had New Jersey license plates. Lupica would later be called by the defense because Richard Hauptmann's car had New York plates. (Courtesy of the Jersey City Free Public Library.)

Many of the servants working for the Lindberghs and Morrows were from Europe. Additionally, police believed that a German had possibly written the ransom notes. Because of this, Maj. Charles Schoeffel of the New Jersey State Police was dispatched to Europe in April 1932. He investigated the backgrounds of the servants and consulted with police agencies on possible suspects. This photograph shows Schoeffel in London. (Courtesy of the New Jersey State Police Museum.)

London, England: April 1932

Henry "Red" Johnson was the boyfriend of Betty Gow, the Lindberghs' nanny. He was a Norwegian sailor who was in the country illegally. Because of his close ties to the family, he was a prime suspect and the first to be arrested. Eventually cleared of suspicion, he was to be deported. However, his deportation warrant was mysteriously nullified, so he left the country of his own free will. (Courtesy of the New Jersey State Police Museum.)

The Jersey City Police played a major role in the kidnapping investigation. They had experienced detectives and were close to New York City. Three major players in the investigation were, from left to right, Det. James Fitzgerald, Det. Robert Coar, and Inspector Harry Walsh. Walsh became the interrogator-in-chief, taking many statements from key suspects. After Violet Sharp committed suicide, he was criticized for his harshness during his questioning of her. (Courtesy of the Jersey City Free Public Library.)

Violet Sharp was a maid at the Morrow estate. She took the phone call from Anne Lindbergh on March 1 when Anne requested that Betty Gow help her at Highfields. A young, flirtatious Englishwoman, she frequently contradicted herself when questioned by the police. Poor health and the stress of repeated harsh interrogations (and some believe a guilty conscience) led her to commit suicide by drinking silver polish that contained cyanide. (Courtesy of the New Jersey State Police Museum.)

Two of the leading investigators were Special Agent Thomas Sisk of the FBI (left) and Det. James Fitzgerald (right) of the Jersey City Police. Sisk complained that the New Jersey State Police tried to push the FBI out of the case. He was heavily involved in the surveillance of Richard Hauptmann's house and in his interrogation after his arrest. (Courtesy of the Jersey City Free Public Library.)

Prior to assisting in the Lindbergh Case, Agent Frank Wilson of the Internal Revenue Department was credited with the downfall of Al Capone on tax evasion. It was upon his insistence that the serial numbers of the ransom bills were recorded, which eventually led to the arrest of Richard Hauptmann. He later served as chief of the Secret Service from 1936 to 1947. (Courtesy of the Historical Society of Princeton.)

Dr. John F. "Jafsie" Condon was the only person to have seen and talked at length with Cemetery John both at Woodlawn and St. Raymond Cemeteries, and he had given several conflicting descriptions of the kidnapper. Here he is reviewing mug shots of criminals in a Bronx police station. Condon had said that he would instantly recognize the kidnapper if he ever saw him again and often claimed to see him walking the streets of the Bronx. After Richard Hauptmann's arrest, Condon viewed him in a police line-up and refused to positively identify him as Cemetery John. In the photograph at left, Condon demonstrates how Cemetery John wore his hat and collar when they met. (Above, courtesy of the Jersey City Free Public Library; left, courtesy of the New Jersey State Police Museum.)

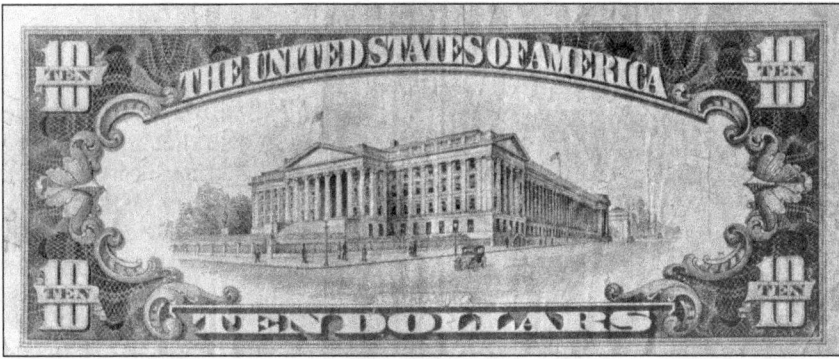

Of the $50,000 ransom, $35,000 was paid in gold certificates. The serial numbers had been recorded and given to banks. Ransom money appeared in circulation within two days of the payoff, but it would be two years before investigators had a solid lead. As an incentive, Charles Lindbergh offered a $2 reward to any bank teller who found ransom money. Finally, in September 1934, a $10 gold certificate (above) appeared in a deposit made by the Warner-Quinlan gas station (below). On the edge of the bill, someone had written a license plate number—4U-13-41. This was the first real break in the case. (Above, courtesy of the Jersey City Free Public Library; below, courtesy of the New Jersey State Police Museum.)

The authorities questioned Walter Lyle, an attendant at the Warner-Quinlan station. He had received a $10 gold certificate in payment for 98¢ worth of gas. Because it was no longer considered legal tender, he feared the bank would not accept the gold certificate, so he scribbled the license plate number of the man who gave it to him on the edge of the bill. He told the police that the man, who spoke with a German accent, said that he had several more gold notes at home. The police traced the license number to a 1930 Dodge sedan owned by Richard Hauptmann. The photograph below shows Walter Lyle standing on top of ladder with fellow employee John Lyons. (Left, courtesy of the New Jersey State Police Museum; below, courtesy of the Jersey City Free Public Library.)

Over the two-and-a-half years since the kidnapping, many people had given descriptions to the police of the person they encountered passing ransom money. The police produced this composite sketch (above) based on those descriptions as well as descriptions made of Cemetery John by Dr. John Condon. Closely resembling the Cemetery John sketch, Bruno Richard Hauptmann (right) was 35 years old at the time of his arrest. Standing five feet nine inches tall, he was of medium build and weighed 180 pounds. He had chestnut-colored hair, blue eyes, and a fair complexion. He was athletic and enjoyed playing soccer. (Both, courtesy of the New Jersey State Police Museum.)

Richard Hauptmann was from Kamenz, Germany, a town in the state of Saxony. In his early years, he had been apprenticed as a carpenter and a machinist. He was a machine gunner during World War I and a petty criminal afterwards. In 1923, after two failed attempts, he successfully entered the United States as a stowaway aboard the SS *Washington*. In America, he occasionally worked as a carpenter. He married Anna Schoeffler in October 1926. On November 3, 1933, Anna Hauptmann gave birth at the Misercordia Hospital on East Eighty-sixth Street in Manhattan to a baby boy that they named Manfred and nicknamed "Bubi." (Left, Courtesy of the Hunterdon County Historical Society; below, courtesy of the Jersey City Free Public Library.)

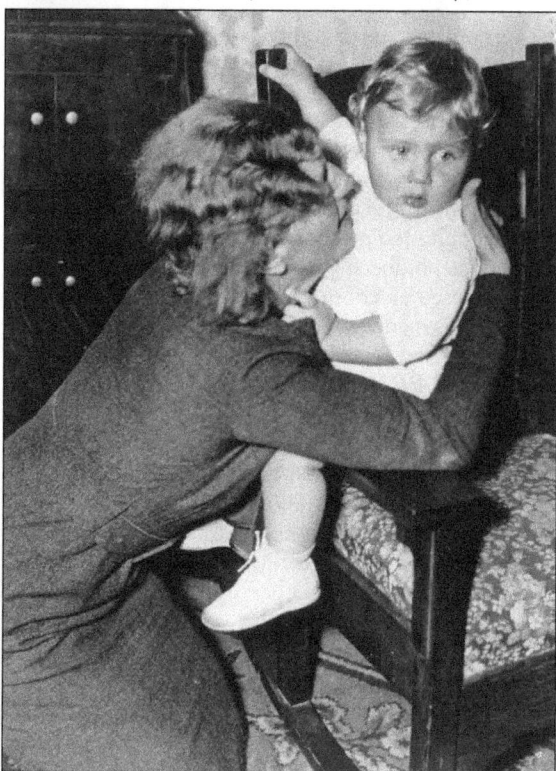

Richard and Anna Hauptmann lived at 1279 East 222nd Street in the Bronx. They had rented the second floor of a two-family house since October 1931. It was a modest apartment with a sitting room, kitchen, two bedrooms, and a bath. Since there was no garage, his landlord gave him permission to build one that he could use rent-free. (Courtesy of Richard Sloan.)

In 1928, Anna Hauptmann visited family in Germany. She is shown here with her mother-in-law, Pauline Hauptmann. Anna's husband, Richard Hauptmann, had a criminal record and had escaped from jail prior to coming to the United States. He had broken into houses and stolen petty cash. He broke into the second-floor window of a house and once, with an accomplice, held up two women at gunpoint. (Courtesy of the New Jersey State Police Museum.)

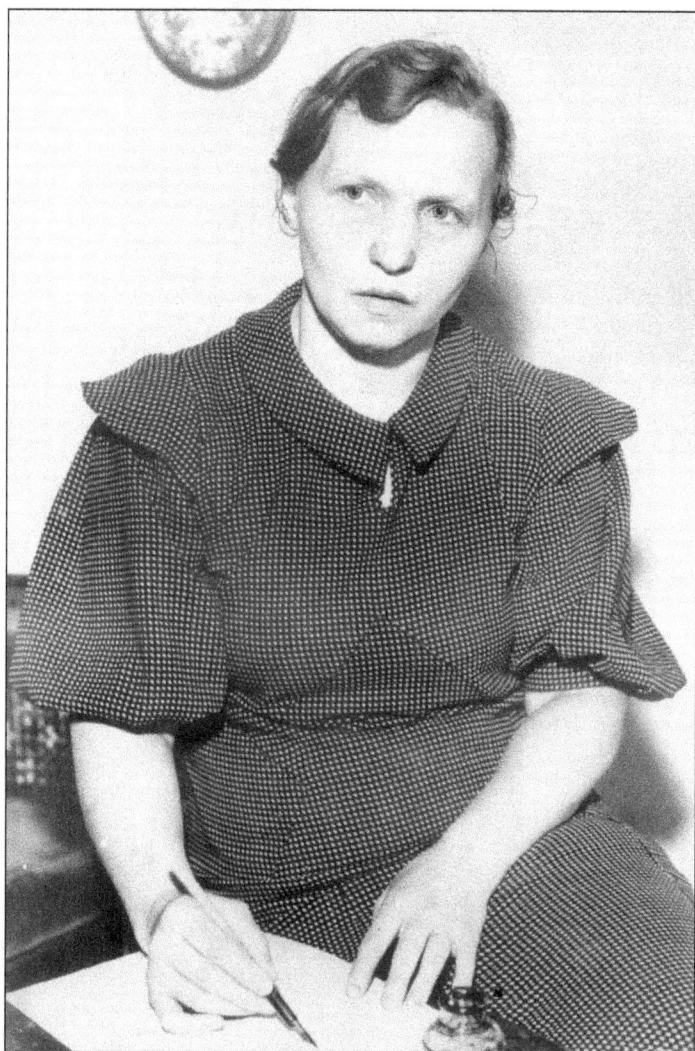

While Richard Hauptmann worked as a carpenter and later as a stock trader, Anna held a full-time job working as a waitress in Frederickson's Bakery in the Bronx. They were a very thrifty family and, in 1931, had saved enough money to take a trip to California to visit Richard's sister Emma Gloeckner, shown above on the far right. Richard and Anna are on the left. Emma (left) had immigrated to the United States in 1908. She was married to Charles Gloeckner, a private chauffeur in Hollywood, California, and had a teenage daughter, Mildred. After the trial, Emma visited her brother at the Death House on May 27, 1935. It was the first time they had seen each other since his visit in 1931. (Above, courtesy of the New Jersey State Police Museum; left, courtesy of Mark W. Falzini.)

Max Rauch (right) and his mother, Pauline Rauch (below), were the Hauptmanns' landlords. The Rauchs did not like the Hauptmanns, especially Richard. They said that he spoke with a very gruff voice and that he was never pleasant to them. They would later testify at his trial that Hauptmann always seemed suspicious. Every time Richard worked in the garage, he closed the door. When he was not around, he kept the garage locked. In the photograph below, Pauline Rauch is denying Richard's defense team access to their apartment because she had just leased it to investigators from the State of New Jersey. (Right, courtesy of the Historical Society of Princeton; below, courtesy of the New Jersey State Police Museum.)

When the police traced the ransom money back to Richard Hauptmann, they staked out his house overnight. The next morning, the New Jersey State Police, New York City Police, Jersey City Police, and FBI followed close behind him as he drove away in this dark blue 1929 Dodge sedan. The plan was to arrest Hauptmann spending ransom money. But he realized he was being followed and tried to get away. Before he could escape, they pulled him over on Gun Hill Road. He was searched, and the contents of his wallet were examined. They found a $20 gold certificate (below). The serial number of the bill matched the listing of Lindbergh ransom money. Hauptmann was immediately arrested. (Both, courtesy of the New Jersey State Police Museum.)

After his arrest, the police thoroughly searched Richard Hauptmann's house. Nothing was found but a few gold certificates that he had already admitted having. One of the investigators allegedly noticed Richard repeatedly glancing out of the window to his garage, which was located across Needham Avenue, a dirt alleyway next to his house. Police began a search of the garage, where they found his carpenter's tools that were missing a 3/4-inch chisel like the one found at the Lindbergh home. After searching for an hour, the police found two packages of 183 ten-dollar gold certificates hidden in the south wall. They literally tore the garage down and discovered an additional 12 packages of gold certificates, all of it Lindbergh ransom money. A total of $13,760 was eventually found hidden in the garage. (Both, courtesy of the New Jersey State Police Museum.)

Richard Hauptmann explained that he had received the money that was found in his garage from his friend and business partner, Isidor Fisch (at left). Hauptmann and Fisch were partners in the fur trading business and stock market. Allegedly, Hauptmann ended up loaning Fisch $7,500. In December 1933, Fisch returned to his native Germany to visit his family. Ailing from tuberculosis, he died on March 29, 1934, in Leipzig. Before leaving, Hauptmann claimed that Fisch gave him several packages to hold for him, including a shoebox that he stored on an upper shelf in his kitchen closet. Months later, after a roof leak damaged the box, Hauptmann discovered money in it. Since Fisch was already dead and owed Hauptmann money, Hauptmann kept out what he was owed and hid the rest in his garage. Below, Isidor Fisch (right) and Richard Hauptmann paddle in Hauptmann's canoe. (Both, courtesy of the New Jersey State Police Museum.)

Richard Hauptmann was taken to the Greenwich Street Police Station, where he was interrogated for 24 hours straight. He contended he was beaten with a hammer in hopes he would confess. He never changed his story about the ransom money or his whereabouts the night of the kidnapping—that he was picking up his wife at the bakery where she worked. Eventually, Hauptmann was booked for extortion. (Courtesy of the New Jersey State Police Museum.)

The police and FBI were elated that they had finally caught their man. Now, the police began jockeying for position, each department wanting to take credit for the arrest. In this photograph are the three top law enforcement officers involved in the investigation. From left to right are J. Edgar Hoover of the FBI; Gen. John J. O'Ryan, New York Police commissioner; and Col. H. Norman Schwarzkopf, New Jersey State Police superintendent. (Courtesy of the New Jersey State Police Museum.)

The authorities wanted Richard Hauptmann extradited to New Jersey, where he could be indicted for the murder of the Lindbergh baby. To do this, they needed a witness to link Hauptmann to the scene of the crime. With the lure of reward money, two witnesses came forward who claimed they saw Hauptmann near the Lindbergh estate around the time of the kidnapping. Millard Whited, an illiterate "mountain man" and habitual liar, claimed he saw Hauptmann wandering around the woods near the Lindbergh estate on two separate occasions. Amandus Hochmuth (above) was a near-blind octogenarian who lived on the outskirts of town. He claimed he was on his porch on March 1, 1932, when he saw Hauptmann, driving a dark sedan with a ladder in it, turn the corner near his house and nearly go into a ditch. The police showed both Hochmuth and Whited photographs of Hauptmann and then asked them to identify him in his jail cell, which they did successfully. (Courtesy of the New Jersey State Police Museum.)

76

The Hunterdon County Grand Jury met twice. During the September 1932 term, the grand jury (pictured above) issued three generic murder indictments for Helen Doe, Richard Doe, and Peter Doe. They met again on October 8, 1934, and took less than a day to issue a murder indictment for Bruno Richard Hauptmann. This paved the way for the extradition proceedings to move forward. Below, from left to right, Bronx district attorney Samuel Foley, Col. H. Norman Schwarzkopf, New Jersey governor A. Harry Moore, and New Jersey attorney general David Wilentz meet in the governor's office to discuss Hauptmann's impending extradition to New Jersey. (Above, courtesy of the New Jersey State Police Museum; below, courtesy of the Jersey City Free Public Library.)

State of New Jersey

EXECUTIVE DEPARTMENT

The Governor of the State of New Jersey

To the Governor of the State of NEW YORK

Whereas: It appears by the papers required by the Statutes of the United States, which are hereunto annexed, and which I certify to be authentic and duly authenticated in accordance with the Laws of this State, that

RICHARD BRUNO HAUPTMANN

stands charged with the crime of HOMICIDE committed in the County of HUNTERDON in this State, and it having been represented to me that HE has fled from the justice of this State and has taken refuge within the State of

NEW YORK

Now Therefore pursuant to the provisions of the Constitution and Laws of the United States in such case made and provided, I do hereby request that the said RICHARD BRUNO HAUPTMANN be apprehended and delivered to CAPTAIN J. J. LAMB who is hereby authorized to receive and convey him to the State of New Jersey there to be dealt with according to Law.

In Testimony Whereof, I have hereunto set my hand and caused the Great Seal of the State to be affixed at Trenton this 20th day of SEPTEMBER in the year of our Lord one thousand nine hundred and thirty-four.

By the Governor:

_____ Governor

_____ Secretary of State

On September 20, 1934, Gov. A. Harry Moore of New Jersey sent an official Executive Request for Extradition of Bruno Richard Hauptmann to the governor of New York. This request led to an extradition hearing in New York before Justice Ernest Hammer beginning on October 16, 1934. On the evening of Friday, October 19, Hauptmann was ushered out of the Bronx County Jail through a crowd of onlookers to awaiting New Jersey state troopers. He was taken with a motorcycle escort to Flemington, New Jersey, to stand trial for the murder of Charles Lindbergh Jr. The circus was soon to begin. (Courtesy of the New Jersey State Police Museum.)

Five

THE PROSECUTION

It had been determined that the murder of Charles Lindbergh Jr. occurred at Highfields, the Lindbergh estate in Hunterdon County. Therefore, the trial of Bruno Richard Hauptmann would take place in Flemington, the county seat. Flemington was a sleepy farming town that was ill equipped for the media circus that was about to descend upon it. Once Hauptmann was extradited from New York in October 1934, the residents of Flemington had scarcely two months to prepare for the biggest trial and news event the town—and country—had ever seen.

Preparations for the media coverage began immediately. Telegraph and telephone wires were run all over town. Two airports were set up on local farms to relay newsreel footage back to New York. All of the spare rooms in Flemington were rented out weeks ahead of the trial.

On January 2, 1935, the Hauptmann trial began, with New Jersey Supreme Court justice Thomas W. Trenchard presiding. Outside the courthouse, thousands of people pushed to get into the building, where only 500 seats were available. At least 150 reporters sat in front on pine boards that allotted them a cramped 18-inch-by-8-inch space. Sheriff John H. Curtiss handed out 500 free tickets for the morning session and 500 for the afternoon. Outside the building, hawkers were selling miniature replica kidnap ladders and alleged locks of the baby's hair.

Security at the courthouse was tight. The New Jersey State Police assigned 16 troopers to the detail. Over the first two days, the jury was selected, all simple country folk who would have their entire lives flashed around the world by the news-hungry press. The prosecution team consisted of David Wilentz, the movie star–looking state attorney general who had never before tried a criminal case; Assistant Attorneys General Joseph Lanigan, Richard Stockton III, and Robert Peacock; Hunterdon County prosecutor Anthony Hauck Jr.; and Special Counsel George Large. Charles Lindbergh, allegedly with a concealed gun in a shoulder holster, sat directly behind the prosecution team along with state police superintendent H. Norman Schwarzkopf. The prosecution was ready.

The Hunterdon County Court House was built in 1828, after an earlier courthouse had burned. It was well suited for Flemington but not for the "Trial of the Century." Telephone and telegraph wires were run all over town in advance of the trial. Most of the wires ran to the Union Hotel, across the street from the courthouse. This was where the press made its unofficial headquarters. (Courtesy of James G. Davidson.)

This view of Main Street in Flemington shows the crowd gathering in front of the courthouse (with the cupola) on January 2, 1935, the opening day of the trial. Just behind the courthouse is the jail where Hauptmann resided in a cramped cell from October 1934 until the conclusion of the trial. (Courtesy of James G. Davidson.)

This view of Main Street is looking towards the south. The pillars of the courthouse can be seen on the far side of the street, and the Union Hotel is just behind the Flemington National Bank sign. Next to the courthouse is the brick hall of records. During the trial, Charles and Anne Lindbergh stayed just outside Flemington at the residence of George Large, a member of the prosecution. (Courtesy of the New Jersey State Police Museum.)

L. Pierre Bottemer was an itinerant artist who sketched images from the Hauptmann trial for the Sunday editions of the *Birmingham News Age-Herald* of Birmingham, Alabama. Pictured are John Walters, chief of Flemington Boro Police (1); L. Pierre Bottemer (2); New Jersey state trooper Walter Schindler (3); news reporter Helen Waterhouse (4); two unidentified reporters (5 and 6); Bertha Robbins (7); and Common Pleas judge Adam O. Robbins (8). (Courtesy of the Hunterdon County Cultural & Historical Commission.)

The second week of the trial saw several inches of snow. Although author H.L. Mencken called the Hauptmann trial "the greatest story since the Resurrection," Flemington farmers still had to get their milk to market. Automobiles could barely get through the near-blizzard conditions, so the locals turned to their old sleighs. Here is a dairy farmer passing by the Hunterdon County Court House on January 24, 1935. (Courtesy of the New Jersey State Police Museum.)

The New Jersey State Police were assigned to assist Flemington with traffic and crowd control during the trial. Journalist Sidney Whipple wrote in *The Lindbergh Crime* that "Sunday found the highways leading into Flemington blocked by a parade of vehicles . . . that extended almost to New York City, moving at the rate of three miles an hour and producing a traffic snarl that a hundred State Police were unable to untangle." (Courtesy of the Hunterdon County Cultural & Historical Commission.)

OFFICIAL PASS

HAUPTMANN TRIAL, Flemington, N. J.

N° 187

MORNING OF

THURSDAY, FEBRUARY 7, 1935

A M

ADMIT ONE

Witness ☐ Press ☐ Photographer ☐ Bar ☐

Present this ticket at the gate between Courthouse and Jail on Court Street. This ticket is not transferable. Must be surrendered on request of the Sheriff.

JOHN H. CURTISS
Sheriff of Hunterdon County

Dated ....

It was very difficult to obtain a pass to the trial. Journalists took up a great number that were given out at each session. Requests for trial passes poured in from politicians, Hollywood and Broadway stars, and society women, as well as the public. The Hauptmann trial became the place to be among the rich and famous. It was the responsibility of Hunterdon County sheriff John H. Curtiss (below right) and Undersheriff Barry Barrowcliff (below left) to maintain order and decorum in the courthouse. Curtiss allowed tourists to have access to the courthouse the first Sunday after the trial began. That day, over 50,000 people showed up to tour both the town and courthouse. (Above, courtesy of James G. Davidson; below, courtesy of the New Jersey State Police Museum.)

Not just adults made up the crowd of curiosity seekers. Juvenile acrobatics came in handy for these three youngsters as they took turns on top of the human pyramid. They were caught looking through the bars of the Flemington jail in hopes of catching a glimpse of Richard Hauptmann. (Courtesy of the New Jersey State Police Museum.)

This was the setting of the "Trial of the Century." The jury box can be seen on the far right. Court reporters sat in front of the judge's bench. The defense sat at the long table on the left and the prosecution on the right. The courthouse was open on the weekends for sightseers. The Rotary Club and American Legion were called in to help with crowd control. (Courtesy of the New Jersey State Police Museum.)

The courtroom became a sea of humanity. There was standing room only, and spectators even took to sitting on the windowsills. Sidney Whipple wrote, "It was the first indication that dignity was in flight and that the circus was coming to town." In this photograph can be seen Anna Hauptmann (9), Richard Hauptmann (14), Charles Lindbergh (18), Col. H. Norman Schwarzkopf (20), David Wilentz (23), and Edward Reilly (24). (Courtesy of the New Jersey State Police Museum.)

This view of the courtroom is looking towards the empty jury box. Sitting just behind the bar is the first line of journalists. They are sitting within earshot of the defendant, Richard Hauptmann (3). Also identified in this photograph are Attorney General David Wilentz (1), New Jersey State Police lieutenant Allan Smith (5), Deputy Sheriff Hovey Low (4), and trooper Hugo Stockburger (5). (Courtesy of the New Jersey State Police Museum.)

An experienced jurist, Justice Thomas Trenchard was very dignified. Fearing a mistrial, he continually sought to keep the courtroom from degenerating into a burlesque show. Commentators felt his treatment of the defense and prosecution was both fair and equal. He was furious when he learned that a microphone had been taped to a fan located over the jury box and a movie camera hidden in the gallery. (Courtesy of the New Jersey State Police Museum.)

This is a photograph of the jury from the trial of Richard Hauptmann. From left to right are (first row) Elmer Smith, Ethel Stockton, Charles Snyder, Verna Snyder, Rosie Pill, and jury foreman Charles Walton; (second row) Robert Cravatt, Philip Hockenbury, George Voorhees, May P. Breslford, Liscome Case, and Howard Briggs. (Courtesy of the New Jersey State Police Museum.)

David Wilentz immigrated to the United States from Latvia and settled in Perth Amboy, New Jersey. Although he had never tried a criminal case, Gov. Harry Moore appointed him attorney general in 1934, and he served until 1944. Afterwards, he established one of the most powerful law firms in New Jersey. In 1950, he helped found the National Democratic Club of New Jersey. He died in 1988 at age 93. (Courtesy of the New Jersey State Police Museum.)

To my friend, Buster
Dave Wilentz

Robert Peacock (left) had been the assistant attorney general of New Jersey for six years and was a member of the prosecution team. His job was to prepare the state's case against Richard Hauptmann. Peacock checked the statements of 310 witnesses and examined 315 documents and exhibits. With him is his friend Judge Robert Carvey. (Courtesy of the New Jersey State Police Museum.)

The prosecution team for the Hauptmann trial consisted of the top jurists in the state. From left to right are (sitting) Hunterdon County prosecutor Anthony M. Hauck, Attorney General David Wilentz, Special Assistant Attorney General George K. Large, and Assistant Attorney General Joseph Lanigan; (standing) Assistant Attorney General Richard Stockton III and Deputy Chief Harry Walsh of the Jersey City Police Department. (Courtesy of the Jersey City Free Public Library.)

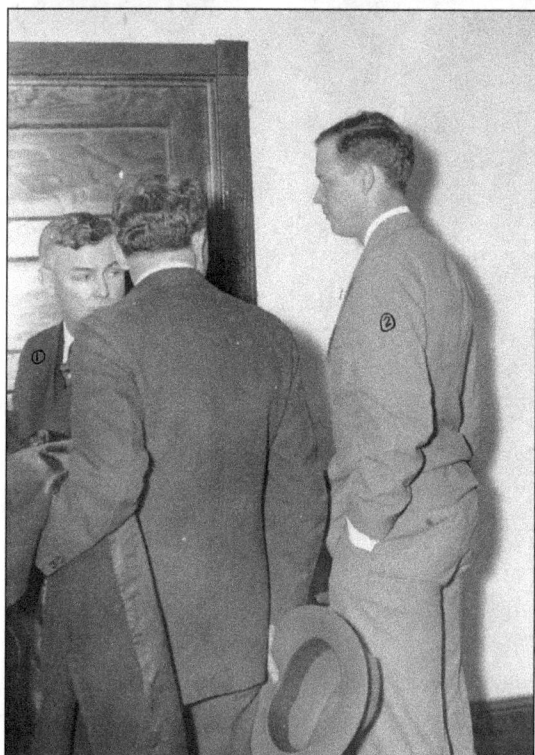

Charles Lindbergh is seen entering the courtroom with Special Assistant Attorney General George K. Large. Lindbergh described the night of the kidnapping and then identified Richard Hauptmann as the man he heard at St. Raymond's Cemetery say "Hey Doctor!" when calling to John Condon. (Courtesy of the Hunterdon County Cultural & Historical Commission.)

Betty Gow (left) testified about the events on the night of the kidnapping and, more importantly, that she had made the undergarments that were used to identify the corpse as the Lindbergh baby. Elsie Whateley (right) was the cook in the Lindbergh home, and her husband, Olly, was the butler. Olly died in 1933, before the trial. Elsie testified but died soon thereafter in 1936. (Courtesy of the New Jersey State Police Museum.)

New York City taxi driver Joseph Perrone identified Richard Hauptmann as the man who gave him a letter, later identified as a ransom note, to deliver to John Condon's house for $1 on the night of March 12, 1932. The note led Condon to a frankfurter stand on Jerome Avenue. Another note found there directed Condon towards Woodlawn Cemetery, where he met with Cemetery John. (Courtesy of the New Jersey State Police Museum.)

Dr. John Condon was the man of mystery and surprises at the trial. Although he had already picked him out of a police lineup, Condon refused to identify Richard Hauptmann as Cemetery John. Once on the witness stand, however, he identified him three times. After the trial, Condon reenacted his role in the Lindbergh Case in department store windows and on the vaudeville stage. (Courtesy of the New Jersey State Police Museum.)

Richard Hauptmann's alibi for being in possession of ransom money was that he had received it from his friend Isidor Fisch, who had died from tuberculosis. Pictured from left to right are Minna Stegnitz, the nurse who tended to Isidor Fisch while he was on his death bed; Assistant Attorney General Richard Stockton III; Detective Arthur Johnson; Czerna and Pinkus Fisch, Isidor's sister-in-law and brother; Assistant Attorney General Robert Peacock; and Isidor's sister Hanna. (Courtesy of the New Jersey State Police Museum.)

It was determined after analyzing the wood used in the construction of the kidnap ladder that it was made from North Carolina pine. Plane marks found on the surface of the wood eventually led investigators to the J.J. Dorn Sawmill in McCormick, South Carolina. The prosecution called to the stand South Carolina state senator Joseph Dorn (at right), who testified that his company shipped the lumber to the National Millwork Company in the Bronx. David Hirsch (below) testified that Richard Hauptmann had purchased some of this wood about the time of the kidnapping. (Both, courtesy of the New Jersey State Police Museum.)

Arthur Koehler was a wood expert who worked for the US Forestry Service in Madison, Wisconsin. He was asked to track down the origin of the wood used in the construction of the kidnap ladder. He checked over 1,500 mills in the South and finally determined that it had come from the Dorn Sawmill. (Courtesy of the New Jersey State Police Museum.)

These are the tools found in Richard Hauptmann's toolbox. Arthur Koehler testified that by using microscopic analysis he was able to match saw and chisel marks on the ladder to Hauptmann's tools. Hauptmann countered that he was a skilled carpenter and that only an unskilled hack could have made such a crude ladder. (Courtesy of the New Jersey State Police Museum.)

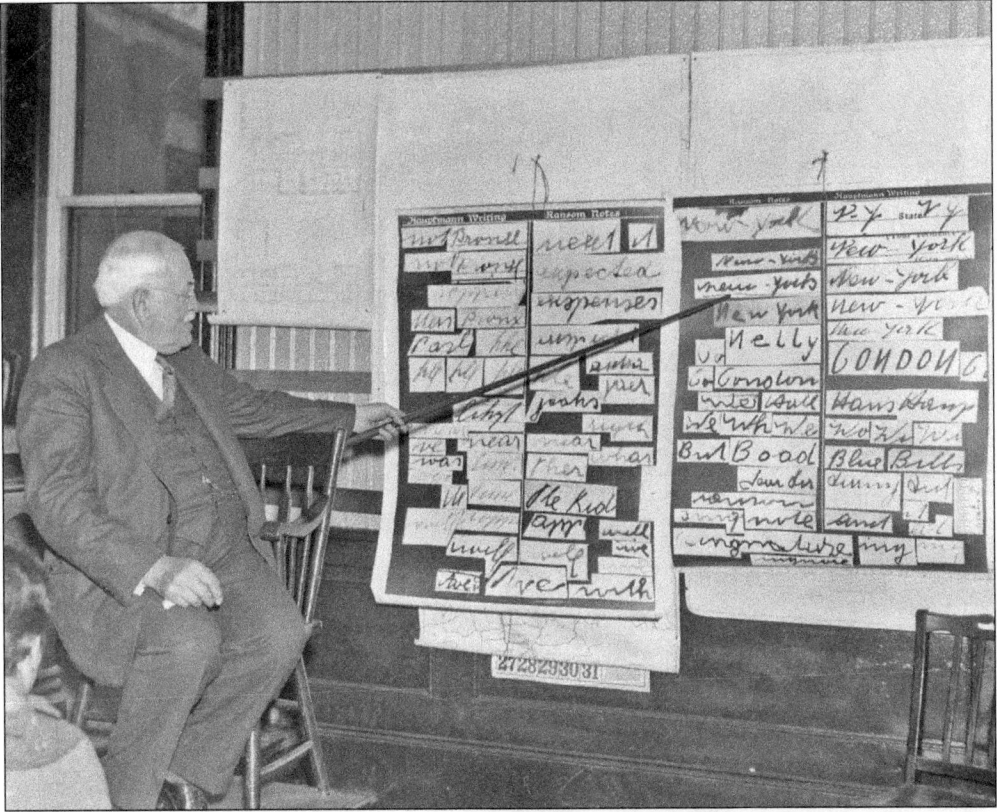

Albert Osborn was one of the most respected experts in handwriting analysis. He and seven others who testified at the trial were considered the "founding fathers" of questioned document examination. They analyzed samples of Richard Hauptmann's writing and agreed that he had written the 15 ransom notes that were sent to the Lindberghs. (Courtesy of the Historical Society of Princeton.)

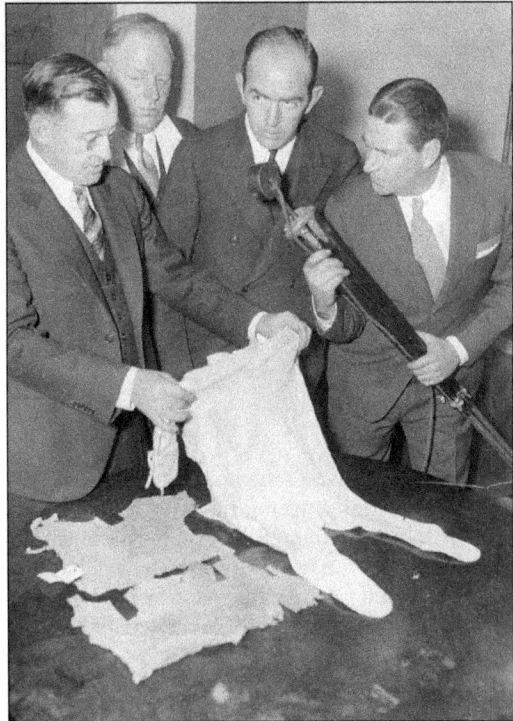

Two key pieces of evidence entered by the prosecution were the Lindbergh baby's clothes. The Dr. Denton's sleeping suit had been sent to Dr. John Condon as proof that the kidnappers had the baby. Betty Gow identified the handmade undershirt found on the corpse as the one she made the night of the kidnapping. Here, Robert Peacock, Capt. John Lamb, and Anthony Hauck show the garments to the press. (Courtesy of the New Jersey State Police Museum.)

NEWS-WEEK

VOL. V, NO. 3   JANUARY 19, 1935   10 CENTS

NELLIE OF FLEMINGTON
(SEE PAGE 7)

During the trial, a young reporter rescued a bedraggled black and white dog from the street and gave her the name Nellie. She became the mascot of the press, and everyone coming to Flemington for the trial wanted to have a picture taken with her. According to the United Press, Nellie received fan mail of over 20 letters and postcards a day. She was also known nationally as the only dog to have a taproom named for her—Nellie's Tap Room in the Union Hotel. There she would visit with her friends, sometimes joining in with a drink of beer! Nellie was even featured on the January 19, 1935, cover of *Newsweek* magazine, shown assisting a New Jersey state trooper while he stands guard. (Courtesy of James G. Davidson.)

Six

THE DEFENSE

Edward J. Reilly was one of the most well known East Coast attorneys. Once a very effective defense attorney, by the time of the Hauptmann trial, he had earned the disparaging moniker of "Death House" Reilly. He was also seen as a fancy city attorney, showing up to court wearing a morning coat, spats, and a carnation. He was not very well liked by the country folk who comprised the jury.

Apparently unaware of this, Richard Hauptmann replaced his initial defense attorney, James Fawcett, with Reilly when he was extradited to New Jersey. William Randolph Hearst, the newspaper magnate, offered Hauptmann a deal: he would pay for Reilly's services provided Anna Hauptmann gave Hearst reporters exclusive access to her. Believing this would be a good way to get their side of the story in the papers, the Hauptmanns agreed.

Second chair to Reilly was local Flemington attorney C. Lloyd "Doc" Fisher. Fisher was the only member of the defense who actually believed Hauptmann was innocent, and the two men became friends. Rounding out the defense team were Frederick A. Pope, an attorney from Somerset County, and Egbert Rosecrans, an attorney and later judge from Warren County.

The defense strategy was simple: to produce witnesses who would corroborate Hauptmann's alibi for the night of the kidnapping and who would corroborate his story regarding how he received the ransom money and cast doubt on the testimonies of Millard Whited, Amandus Hochmuth, and the handwriting experts. The defense would also press that the kidnapping was an inside job, thereby casting doubt on Betty Gow and the deceased Violet Sharp.

Meanwhile, by the second week of the trial, the sleepy town of Flemington was in a complete frenzy. Mobs of the rich and famous as well as local citizens had arrived. Film crews clogged the streets. A sea of spent flashbulbs from cameras littered the sidewalks. The press hung on every word being said inside the courtroom and every rumor circulating outside. The defense was now ready to present its case.

David Wilentz (left) and Edward Reilly seem happy, friendly, and courteous in this staged photograph. Although inexperienced in a courtroom, Wilentz and his team were much better prepared and had nearly unlimited funds for their investigation, while the defense team was financially strapped. Reilly seemed nonchalant about the trial and Richard Hauptmann's fate. Many said he spoke down to the jury and considered them "country bumpkins." (Courtesy of the Hunterdon County Cultural & Historical Commission.)

Edward Reilly was often putting himself in front of the camera. In this photograph, he is seen posing with some Flemington locals and the famous press mascot Nellie. Those shown are, from left to right, Emma Ewing (1), Alice Johnson (2), Edward Reilly (3), Nellie (4), Elizabeth Kerr (5), and Manuel Papas (6). (Courtesy of the Hunterdon County Cultural & Historical Commission.)

Edward Reilly went so far as to have special letterhead made for the trial. It is said that he used it to reply to fan mail. Embossed in red ink, note the three-section kidnap ladder and his address at the Union Hotel. At Reilly's request, veteran composing room foreman Hank Reamer and Howard Moreau, the editor and publisher of the *Hunterdon County Democrat*, designed the letterhead. (Courtesy of the New Jersey State Police Museum.)

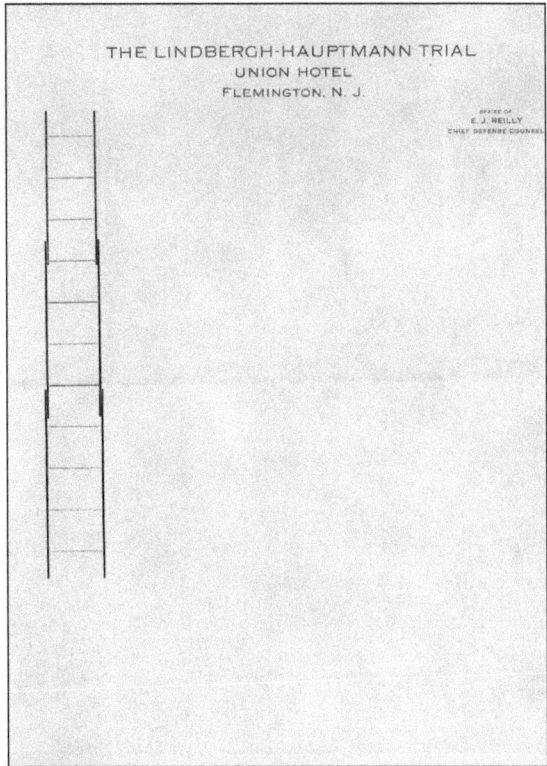

THE LINDBERGH-HAUPTMANN TRIAL
UNION HOTEL
FLEMINGTON, N. J

OFFICE OF
E. J. REILLY
CHIEF DEFENSE COUNSEL

Although married, Edward Reilly was known to attend the trial with a bevy of attractive secretaries. They would mysteriously disappear when his wife would attend the trial. Reilly was known to have often smelled of alcohol and one night was reported to have danced around the flagpole in front of the courthouse. (Courtesy of the New Jersey State Police Museum.)

Richard Hauptmann confers with defense attorney Egbert Rosecrans. Rosecrans was born in Hoboken in 1890. By 1920, he was practicing law in Blairstown, New Jersey. After the Hauptmann trial, he returned to Warren County, where he was appointed a judge, a position he held until his death in 1948. (Courtesy of the New Jersey State Police Museum.)

Another member of the defense team was Frederick Pope. Both Pope and Egbert Rosecrans were related to famous Civil War generals. Pope admitted that he joined the defense for the publicity, and his first condition for joining was that he was to be paid. Immediately after the trial, Pope was conferred as a judge in Somerset County. He died in 1957 at age 80. (Courtesy of the New Jersey State Police Museum.)

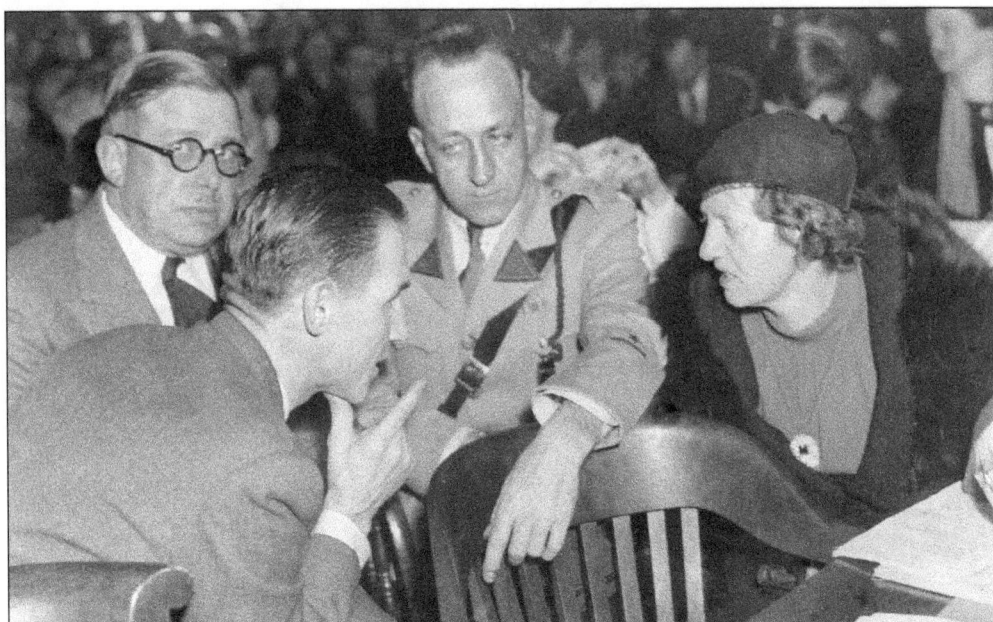

Deputy Sheriff Hovey P. Low (left) looks on with New Jersey state trooper Alan Smith while Richard and Anna Hauptmann converse in German. Stockburger had been on the force for five years when the trial began. Born in Germany and fluent in German, he was detailed to guard Hauptmann from noon to 6:00 p.m. every day and document anything the Hauptmanns said in German. (Courtesy of the New Jersey State Police Museum.)

C. Lloyd Fisher had his law office across the street from the courthouse in Flemington. He practiced law there his entire life and only lived a few blocks away. He was a very popular lawyer with the locals. Here, he consults with Anna Hauptmann and her cousin Harry Whitney. (Courtesy of the New Jersey State Police Museum.)

Unlike Edward Reilly, Lloyd Fisher took his role seriously and tried to prepare the best possible defense for his client. After Richard Hauptmann was convicted, he fired Reilly and had Fisher file his appeal. In 1937, Gov. Harold Hoffman appointed Fisher the Hunterdon County prosecutor, replacing Anthony Hauck. Fisher died in 1960 at the age of 63. He believed Hauptmann was innocent to the end. (Courtesy of the New Jersey State Police Museum.)

Getting ready for another day in court are, from left to right, New Jersey State Police corporal Cornelius O'Donnell, Edward Reilly, Richard Hauptmann, Deputy Sheriff Hovey Low, Lloyd Fisher, and Egbert Rosecrans. (Courtesy of the New Jersey State Police Museum.)

Cpl. Cornelius O'Donnell is leading
Richard Hauptmann through the
courtroom, followed by Deputy Sheriff
Hovey Low and Lt. Alan Smith.
Each day at the trial, Hauptmann
looked his best. This was thanks to
local tailor Ben Karrow, who would
take Hauptmann's suit and press it
for him each night. (Courtesy of the
New Jersey State Police Museum.)

Richard Hauptmann received several
checks for $1 that he naively believed
were sent by supporters wishing
to contribute to his defense fund.
He later learned that they simply
wanted his autograph from the
endorsement. He also autographed
the back of a trial pass for Hunterdon
County sheriff John H. Curtiss and
this photograph for his attorney
Lloyd Fisher. (Courtesy of the New
Jersey State Police Museum.)

Anna Hauptmann confers with James Rao, Edward Reilly's investigator. During the trial, Anna Hauptmann was kept isolated from the public, and a house was rented for her in Flemington where the *New York Journal* provided guards for her protection. On the weekends, she would return to the Bronx, where she stayed with friends and saw her son Manfred. (Courtesy of the New Jersey State Police Museum.)

Edward Reilly leaves his office in the Union Hotel with defense witness Anna Bonesteel. Bonesteel owned a restaurant in Yonkers and testified that on the night of the kidnapping, she saw Violet Sharp in her restaurant with a baby in her arms. Attorney General David Wilentz quickly discredited her testimony. (Courtesy of the Hunterdon County Cultural & Historical Commission.)

Elvert Carlstrom was another witness for the defense. He testified that he saw Richard Hauptmann in Fredericksen's Bakery on the night of the kidnapping. Carlstrom said that he specifically remembered him because Hauptmann had made fun of his accent. David Wilentz effectively destroyed Carlstrom's credibility by calling his memory into question. (Courtesy of the New Jersey State Police Museum.)

Hans Kloppenburg was Richard Hauptmann's best friend. Tall and slender, he stood six feet two inches tall with grey eyes and thinning hair. Hans claimed that he saw Isidor Fisch give Hauptmann the box that allegedly contained ransom money. A few days before he was to testify on Hauptmann's behalf, Attorney General David Wilentz threatened to charge Hans as an accessory if he testified about the box. (Courtesy of Mark W. Falzini.)

Seated at the table are the handwriting experts hired by the defense. According to the FBI, the prosecution's expert, Albert Osborn, did not say conclusively that Richard Hauptmann wrote all 15 ransom notes until the police told him that they found ransom money in his garage. John M. Treandley was the only handwriting expert to agree to testify on Hauptmann's behalf. (Courtesy of the New Jersey State Police Museum.)

Walter Winchell was the most celebrated and influential radio personality and columnist of the time. He wrote for the *New York Daily Mirror* and was the first syndicated gossip columnist to have his column appear in 2,000 newspapers every day. In 1930, he joined WABC radio. He reached an astounding 50 million people through his columns and radio program. He is shown here with novelist Fannie Hurst. (Courtesy of the New Jersey State Police Museum.)

Realizing that the trial of Richard Hauptmann would be one of the most important trials of the century, editors sent their best reporters and photographers to cover it. Famed photographer Margaret Bourke-White covered the Hauptmann trial for *Fortune* magazine, which had hired her as its first female photographer in 1929. Later, Henry Luce hired her as the first female photographer for *Life* magazine. She became the first female war correspondent during World War II, covering the German invasion of the Soviet Union, and was later reassigned to travel with Gen. George Patton. She was also one of the photographers who documented the Nazi death camps. Two of her most famous photographs were of Mohandas K. Gandhi at his spinning wheel and of Soviet leader Josef Stalin smiling. Her photographs can be seen in museums in New York and Cleveland as well as the Library of Congress. (Courtesy of the New Jersey State Police Museum.)

Pool photographers were assigned to photograph the trial for the myriad of newspapers and press agencies covering it. It was common for news agencies to pool their resources to avoid duplication in their coverage. The photographers had their headquarters and darkroom located in a bakery near the courthouse on Bloomfield Avenue. Unfortunately, the names of the photographers are unknown. (Both, courtesy of the New Jersey State Police Museum.)

Dice, pitching pennies, and checkers were the most common games played by the press during breaks in the trial or at night. While awaiting the verdict, a dice game was held in the courthouse library. According to one witness, the pot had gotten to $880 when someone saw Judge Thomas Trenchard approaching. The players quickly grabbed law books and appeared to be innocently reading when Trenchard entered the room. (Courtesy of the New Jersey State Police Museum.)

As the trial progressed, more and more people came to Flemington. Several local schoolteachers managed to obtain passes for their classes to attend a session of the trial. Here, curious students are attempting to catch a glimpse of Richard Hauptmann as he is being taken from the courtroom to his jail cell. (Courtesy of the New Jersey State Police Museum.)

A guest is attempting to register in the lobby of the Union Hotel. Notice the model of the courthouse above the telephone booth to the right. Behind the back and right walls is the large dining room. The hotel was built in the 1870s. It had four floors and 50 rooms. The jury was sequestered on the fourth floor but "exercised" on the balcony of the second floor—always while under guard. The above photograph was taken during the day, while the trial was in session. The photograph below was taken at night, after the court recessed for the day. The hotel manager, Walter Boyd, is in the foreground. (Both, courtesy of the New Jersey State Police Museum.)

Nellie's Tap Room was an additional bar set up in the Union Hotel to cater to thirsty patrons during breaks in the trial and after court recessed for the day. In this photograph, bartender Eary Gray is serving a local patron during a lull in activity. Note the spittoons on the floor along the bar. (Courtesy of the New Jersey State Police Museum.)

Each day after the court recessed, the jurors would make their way single file and under guard from the courthouse to the Union Hotel, where they were sequestered. From left to right are Constable Oden Baggstrom, jury foreman Charles Walton Sr., Rosie Pill, Verna Snyder, Charles Snyder, Elmer Smith, Robert Cravatt, George Voorhees, Constable Clarence Doane, Matron Francis Robbinson, Matron Susan Dilts, and Matron Pearl Conover. (Courtesy of the Hunterdon County Cultural & Historical Commission.)

The weather during the six-week trial was very cold and snowy. Above, the New Jersey Highway Department is shown plowing the roads so the news dispatches could get to the airport just north of town near present-day Packers Island. O.J. Whitney was one of many pilots who flew the dispatches from Flemington to Newark. From there they were driven to the newspaper offices in New York City. (Both, courtesy of the New Jersey State Police Museum.)

Seven

THE VERDICT

After 33 days, the prosecution and defense rested their cases. Judge Thomas Trenchard charged the jury and explained their verdict options: acquittal, guilty with mercy (life imprisonment), or guilty with the penalty of death. At 11:15 a.m. on February 13, 1935, the jury retired to decide the fate of Richard Hauptmann. Spectators were evicted from the courthouse, and the doors were locked. Only law enforcement, clerks, and 150 reporters were allowed to remain, locked inside until the jury returned.

As time dragged on, crowds began to gather outside. The press devised ways to communicate the verdict with reporters outside. By mistake, an erroneous signal by the Associated Press went out, and instantly, incorrect headlines were printed in newspapers around the country.

Finally, at 10:38 p.m. the old courthouse bell tolled, announcing that the jury had returned a verdict. Outside, floodlights and flares were set up for the movie cameras. The crowd was so great that no one could move. The verdict was murder in the first degree with a sentence of death. The date of the execution was set for the week of March 18.

But the story was not over. New Jersey governor Harold Hoffman felt there were too many unanswered questions. As Hauptmann's attorneys filed their appeals, Governor Hoffman granted Hauptmann a 30-day stay of execution. Investigators working for the governor tried to uncover new facts. Hauptmann still refused to confess but volunteered to take a lie detector test that the New Jersey legislature refused to authorize. As Hoffman's reinvestigation continued, calls for his impeachment began to be heard.

Meanwhile, the Court of Error and Appeals refused to overturn the Flemington verdict. Hauptmann's last hope was the US Supreme Court, which refused to even hear the case. After a year of appeals, time had run out. On Friday, April 3, 1936, with searchlights flashing across the crowds of people outside the Trenton State Prison, Bruno Richard Hauptmann was executed in the electric chair. Hauptmann never confessed, swearing to the end he was innocent.

A staff correspondent for the *New York Times* wrote on February 14, 1935, that outside the courthouse, "there were thousands of persons in the throng, perhaps as many as 6,000 or 7,000. They swarmed all over the street, completely blocking traffic on Main Street. . . . At 10:27, Keith Barrowcliff, a deputy sheriff, climbed up into the belfry of the courthouse and rang the century-old bell, which signaled that the jurors had come to a decision, a swelling shout went up from the throng. Cameramen turned night into day with flares . . . the loud reports of the exploding flashbulbs made a hollow alien echo within the tense courtroom where a man waited for a sentence of death. . . . The verdict was pronounced, and . . . a great shout went up from outside and the throng pressed closer to the building." (Above, courtesy of the Jersey City Free Public Library; left, courtesy of the New Jersey State Police Museum.)

Several minutes before the actual jury verdict was read, an Associated Press correspondent erroneously sent a signal out of the courthouse that Hauptmann was found guilty with a sentence of life imprisonment. Eager to scoop their rivals, thousands of AP-affiliated newspapers, including the *Erie Dispatch-Herald*, immediately printed the false report in extra editions of their newspapers. They were quickly distributed to newsstands around the country with hawkers pushing the papers to passersby with the traditional shouts of "Extra! Extra! Read all about it!" The following morning, the correct headlines were printed as well as a front-page article providing an explanation for the error. (Both, courtesy of the New Jersey State Police Museum.)

LAST DAY OF TRIAL

HUNTERDON COUNTY
COURT HOUSE
FLEMINGTON, N. J.
SCENE OF THE FAMOUS
LINDBERGH KIDNAPPING TRIAL
1935

William Sauter Jr.,
10 Pelham Rd.,
Phila. Penna.

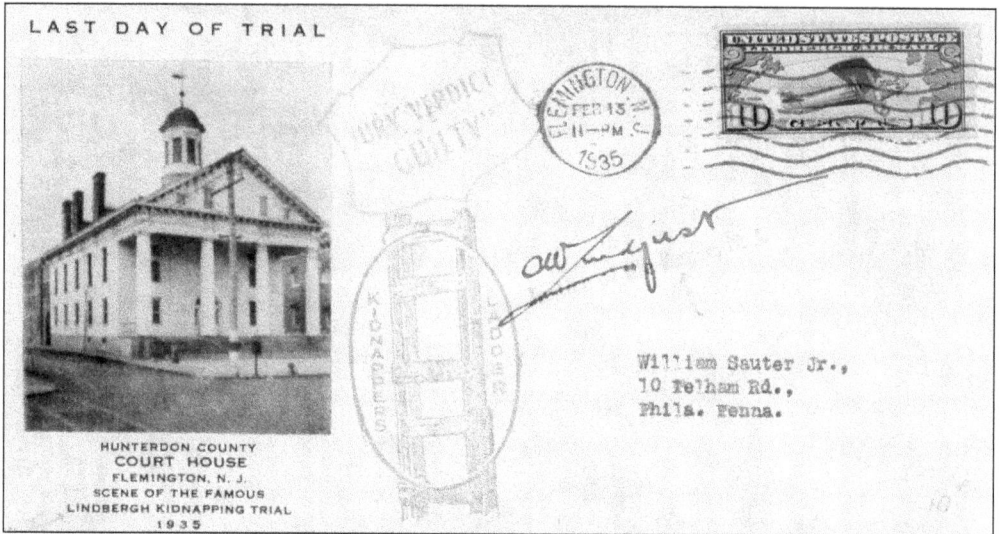

As the verdict was read, the town temporarily celebrated, then the crowds faded and Nellie's Tap Room grew empty. Except for the large piles of trash left on the streets and sidewalks, Flemington returned to being a sleepy farming town. The last souvenir of the trial was this postal cachet, one of 300 made and postmarked just 30 minutes after the guilty verdict was announced. (Courtesy of James G. Davidson.)

Justice Thomas Trenchard received large amounts of fan mail congratulating him on the verdict. However, not everyone was happy that Richard Hauptmann was found guilty and sentenced to die. Most of the mail Trenchard received criticized his charge to the jury or his general handling of the case. This threatening letter was anonymously mailed to him on February 20, 1935, from Newark, New Jersey. (Courtesy of the New Jersey State Police Museum.)

114

After hearing the verdict, Richard Hauptmann was led back to his cell, where he cried almost the entire night. The following day, February 14, 1935, he was transferred to Death Row in the New Jersey State Prison on Cass Street in Trenton. Security was tight, and his new cell was just yards from the room that housed the electric chair. (Courtesy of the Hunterdon County Historical Society.)

Richard and Anna Hauptmann immediately fired attorney Edward Reilly. Reilly returned to New York City and, during a bitter divorce in 1937, was committed to Kings Park State Hospital for about a year with a mental breakdown. He died on Christmas Day, 1946. Hauptmann now turned to his friend Lloyd Fisher, shown here, to begin the appeal process. (Courtesy of the New Jersey State Police Museum.)

On January 15, 1935, Chief Justice Thomas J. Brogan swore in Harold G. Hoffman as the 41st governor of New Jersey. From 1931 to 1935, Hoffman served as the commissioner of motor vehicles, and he had followed the Lindbergh Case closely and knew many of the participants. After taking office, Hoffman expressed doubts about the prosecution's case and, in addition to ordering the state police to revisit the case, began his own reinvestigation. Breaking state law, Hoffman visited Richard Hauptmann in the state prison on October 16, 1935, and granted him a 30-day stay of execution. Because the public perceived that he believed Hauptmann was innocent and, more importantly, because of his advocacy for a state sales tax, Hoffmann was not reelected. (Both, courtesy of the New Jersey State Police Museum.)

After Hauptmann's conviction, his case was sent to the New Jersey Court of Error and Appeals, which refused to overturn his conviction. Gov. Harold Hoffman then ordered the Board of Pardons to review his case. Here, members of the board are on their way to the hearing of Hauptmann's plea for a commutation of the death sentence. From back to front are Joseph Deer, a Jersey City newspaper publisher; William LeGay, the governor's private secretary (and not a board member); Gov. Harold Hoffman; William Volfskiel, a lawyer from Elizabeth; Harold Wells, a lawyer from Bordentown; George van Buskirk, a businessman from Hackensack; and Walter Hetfield, a lawyer from Plainfield. (Courtesy of the New Jersey State Police Museum.)

Richard Hauptmann's appeals to the Court of Error and Appeals, the Board of Pardons, and the US Supreme Court had postponed his execution. As the new execution date, March 31, 1936, approached, he once again appealed to the governor for a reprieve. However, the governor did not have the legal authority to grant one. Here, Harold Hoffman's secretary, R. William LeGay, reads the governor's reprieve denial to the press. (Courtesy of the New Jersey State Police Museum.)

Security surrounding the Death House at the state prison was tight. Trenton City Police and state troopers were brought in to assist the prison guards. The entrance of the Death House, shown here, has an Egyptian theme, complete with papyrus-styled columns and engraved hieroglyphics. Egyptian Revivalism was a popular architectural style in the 19th century. John Haviland, an English-born architect working in Philadelphia, designed the facade in the 1830s. (Courtesy of Oliver Sissman.)

Thousands of people waited outside the prison for the execution to take place. As the crowds grew, another postponement was declared, and the execution was finally set for April 3, 1936. Two local Trenton hotels, the Stacey Trent and Hildebrecht, held execution parties. Close to 10,000 people turned out for the execution. Mounted troopers were used to help keep the crowd on Second Street, two blocks away from the prison. (Courtesy of the Hunterdon County Historical Society.)

Witnesses to the execution underwent rigorous scrutiny before they were allowed in the execution chamber. They had to walk through lines of guards and then, with their hands aloft, they were searched. This occurred four times as they made their way through the prison walls to the Death House. Guards were especially looking for hidden cameras. In 1928, Tom Howard, a photographer working for the *New York Daily News*, had smuggled a small camera attached to his ankle into Sing Sing Prison and photographed the execution of Ruth Snyder. The photographs were published the following day. Mark Kimberling, the warden of the New Jersey State Prison, was determined not to allow this to happen with this execution. (Both, courtesy of the Hunterdon County Historical Society.)

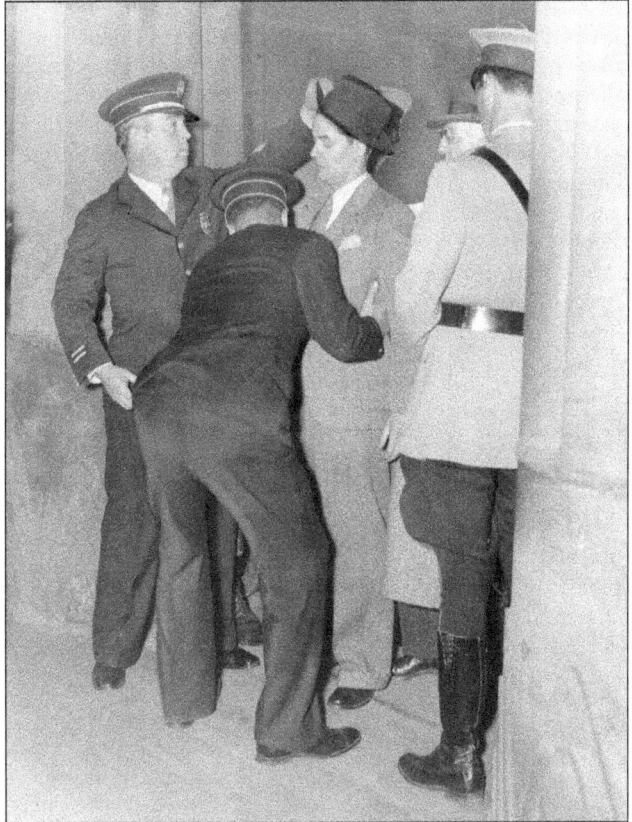

Just as Lindbergh's garage had been turned into a makeshift police headquarters during the initial investigation, the Trenton State Prison's garage had been turned into a makeshift pressroom. Telegraph and telephone lines were installed to get word out to the public as soon as the execution occurred. Reporters who had covered the trial were now covering the execution. Gabriel Heatter, who would later become famous for his World War II catchphrase "There's good news tonight!", caught his big break in broadcasting when he covered the trial and execution of Richard Hauptmann. Heatter was live on the air at 8:00 p.m. expecting Hauptmann to be executed on time. However, there was a 47-minute delay, during which time he was forced to ad-lib to his audience while awaiting confirmation of Hauptmann's death. (Both, courtesy of the Hunterdon County Historical Society.)

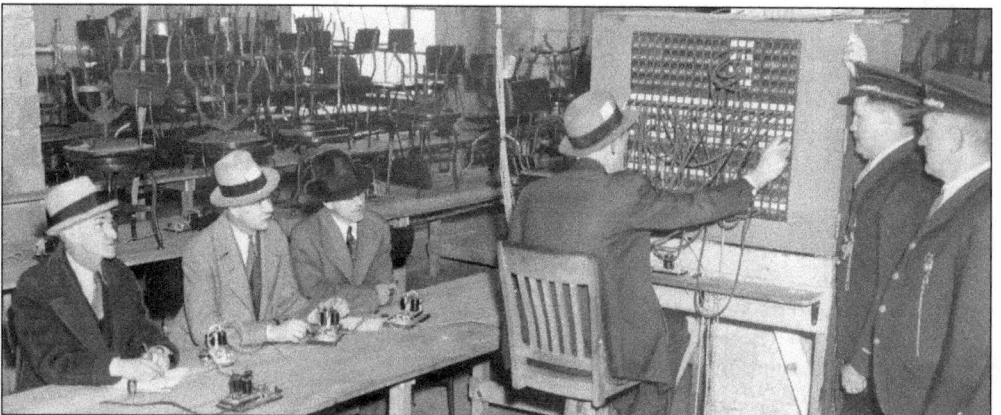

Although reporters were allowed in the execution chamber, cameras were not. Therefore, sketch artists were employed to draw renditions of Richard Hauptmann's last moments. This sketch, by a *Daily News* sketch artist, shows Hauptmann being led to the electric chair by his spiritual advisor, Rev. John Matthiessen of the Trinity Lutheran Church in Trenton, New Jersey. (Courtesy of the New Jersey State Police Museum.)

Another artist present was Sara Wolf, who received $150 for her drawings. This sketch depicts the sight that met Dr. Charles Mitchell, one of the witnesses. He wrote that Richard Hauptmann "lurched into the death chamber. He walked like an automaton. His close clipped head; deep-sunken eyes and his pallid features had already taken on the appearance of a cadaver. He had lost 30 pounds [and] he stared out into space." (Courtesy of the Hunterdon County Historical Society.)

Electric Chair at State Prison, Trenton, N.J.

On March 1, 1907, New Jersey passed a law authorizing execution by electrocution, thus becoming only the third state in the nation to adopt electrocution as its form of capital punishment. Until that time, most states hanged condemned prisoners. Carl Adams, the founder of Adams Electric in Hamilton Township, New Jersey, built this electric chair, known as "Old Sparkey." It has heavy leather straps to lash each leg at the ankle, two straps for each arm, and straps on the waist, head, and chest. The chair has an adjustable armrest, backrest, and headrest, allowing for a last few minutes of comfort. The first execution took place on December 12, 1907, and the last on January 22, 1963. Richard Hauptmann was the 117th out of 160 condemned prisoners to die in New Jersey's electric chair. (Above, courtesy of Richard Sloan; left, courtesy of the New Jersey State Police Museum.)

The execution of Bruno Richard Hauptmann was carried out at 8:47 p.m. on the night of April 3, 1936. No sooner had word been given of his death than the throngs of spectators immediately dispersed. The following day, they returned for one last look as the hearse containing Hauptmann's body left the prison. (Courtesy of the Hunterdon County Historical Society.)

A police escort followed the hearse from Trenton to a funeral parlor at Fifty-second Street and Lexington Avenue in New York City. From there, Richard Hauptmann's body was taken during the night to the Fresh Pond Crematory in Middle Village, Long Island. Along the way, Hauptmann's body was transferred to a second hearse in an attempt to evade spectators. (Courtesy of the Hunterdon County Historical Society.)

On April 6, 1936, Richard Hauptmann's remains were taken into the Fresh Pond Crematory, where Anna Hauptmann and a handful of family and close friends were waiting. New Jersey law did not allow a public funeral for an executed felon, so Anna Hauptmann had to agree not to hold a public funeral in order to get her husband's body out of state. (Courtesy of the Hunterdon County Historical Society.)

There was nothing to see, and no announcement was to be made. Yet the ever-present crowd of approximately 2,000 spectators gathered once again. This time, they waited across the street from the Fresh Pond Crematory in hopes of catching a glimpse of the funeral. In the funeral chapel, Anna Hauptmann and 28 others listened to eulogies by Rev. D.G. Werner and Rev. John Matthiessen, her husband's spiritual advisors. (Courtesy of the Hunterdon County Historical Society.)

This is the first page of Richard Hauptmann's last letter that he ever wrote. It was to Gov. Harold G. Hoffman on March 31, 1936, the day he was supposed to die in the electric chair. It reads in part, "Your Excellence: My writing is not for fear of losing my life, this is in the hands of God, it is His will. I will go gladly, it means the end of my tremendous suffering. Only in thinking of my wife and my little boy, that is breaking my heart. I know until this terrible crime is solvet, they will have to suffer unter the weight of my unfair conviction. . . . Please investigate, because the case is not solvet, it only adds another death to the Lindbergh case. I thank your Excellence, from the bottom of my heart, and may God bless you, Respectfully, Bruno Richard Hauptmann." He later went on to say, "They think when I die, the case will die. They think it will be like a book I close. But the book, it will never close." (Courtesy of the New Jersey State Police Museum.)

EPILOGUE

In December 1935, Charles and Anne Lindbergh moved to England to escape the American media. There they were able to live a near-normal life away from the prying eyes of the press. In a 1990 interview for *The American Experience*, Anne Lindbergh described their time in England as "very nice. It was very normal. Nobody bothered us. We weren't anybody to them, really. It was a very happy, normal life. Wonderful, really."

They returned shortly before the outbreak of World War II, and Charles Lindbergh became the spokesman for the America First Movement, an isolationist organization. Lindbergh's antiwar stance turned most of the public against him, and his popularity plummeted. When Japan attacked Pearl Harbor, however, Lindbergh resigned from the America First organization and assisted with the war effort in the Pacific theater. After the war, he became a proponent of the environmentalist movement. He died in 1974 at his home in Hawai'i at the age of 72.

Anne Morrow Lindbergh became a prolific author, publishing her diaries and letters as well as books of poetry. She also trained as a pilot and navigator and assisted her husband on many of his flights. She died in 2001 at the age of 94.

Anna Hauptmann eventually moved from the Bronx to Lancaster County, Pennsylvania, where she lived until her death in 1994 at age 95. Like her husband, she was cremated, and her remains were scattered in Germany. She spent her life convinced of her husband's innocence and tried unsuccessfully to have his conviction overturned.

Eighty years after the kidnapping, interest in the "Crime of the Century" has not waned. At the New Jersey State Police Museum in West Trenton, New Jersey, evidence from the Hauptmann trial is on public display. In 1981, New Jersey governor Brendan Byrne issued an executive order declaring that all of the police files pertaining to the Lindbergh Kidnapping investigation would be made available for research. Today, in the New Jersey State Police Museum's archive, the public has free access to over a quarter of a million documents, photographs, and videos pertaining to the case that never dies.

BIBLIOGRAPHY

Berg, A. Scott. *Lindbergh*. New York: G.P. Putnam's Sons, 1998.

Falzini, Mark W. *Their Fifteen Minutes: Biographical Sketches of the Lindbergh Case*. New York: iUniverse, Inc., 2008.

Fisher, Jim. *The Lindbergh Case*. New Brunswick, NJ: Rutgers University Press, 1987.

Gardner, Lloyd C. *The Case That Never Dies*. New Brunswick, NJ: Rutgers University Press, 2004.

Herrmann, Dorothy. *Anne Morrow Lindbergh: A Gift For Life*. New York: Penguin Books, 1993.

Hertog, Susan. *Anne Morrow Lindbergh: Her Life*. New York: Anchor, 1999.

Kennedy, Ludovic. *The Airman and the Carpenter*. New York: Viking, 1985.

Mitchell, Charles H. "Did Hauptmann Die in the Chair?" *Daring Detective* 4, no. 21 (June 1936).

Waller, George. *Kidnap: The Story of the Lindbergh Case*. New York: The Dial Press, 1961.

Whipple, Sidney B. *The Lindbergh Crime*. New York: Blue Ribbon Books, 1935.

Visit us at
arcadiapublishing.com